# THE
# MANTLE
## —— OF ——
# JOSEPH

## BRYAN WEBB

Edited by Evangelist Meta Townsand

Oracle Publishing

# Dedication

*"...But as for you, ye thought evil against me; but God meant it unto good, to bring to pass, as it is this day, to save much people alive."*

—Joseph
Genesis 50:20 KJV

This book would not be possible if it had not been for the blessing of just a handful of people. I first would like to dedicate this book to Jesus Christ. Like Joseph, so many people wrote me off—Jesus never did. He encouraged me when I couldn't encourage myself. When people called me crazy, He gave me the gift to write, not for myself, but for the empowering of others, which is the sole reason why I wrote this book. He opened my eyes to the reality of my dreams. He shut the doors to people and opportunities that would ultimately hinder my dreams from coming to pass. He allowed me to establish those endeavors that would only bless others. He also sealed me with His prophetic approval, and allowed me to see that I don't need man to affirm my dreams. It is through Him that I realized ministry is not just preaching to people, it's mustering up the self-sacrifice to help others actualize their dreams—even when you are taken for granted or left to what people mistake as false motives and hidden agendas.

The second person I would like to dedicate this book to is my wife, Kristy Lewis-Webb. My wife, despite the many trials and challenges we have faced in life, has never wavered from her love and devotion to me. She has loved me, and devoted herself to me, when even her most trusted companions gave her advice to the contrary. She has been my teacher of faith, illuminating me to the fact that when God says it, then there is no debate—it is so. Her unwavering faith and resolute belief in what God has promised her has made me stubborn enough to believe in myself, my dreams and my marriage. What she sees in me is anyone's guess. I must be doing something right. Kristy, thank you so much. You are a great woman of God, and I cannot wait to see what else the Lord is going to do through you for the benefit of His people.

Lastly, I would like to dedicate this book to my children— Joshua, Jeremiah, Janyce and Josiah. My family is truly the reason why I strive for more. When I am depressed, they give me laughter. At the end of a tough day of trials and tribulations, my children give me the blessed assurance that life is so much more than my frailties and short comings. The tireless days of preparing dinner, helping with homework, putting them to bed, doing laundry, ironing clothes and getting them up for church, while finding time to write this book, was all too worth the effort. Thank you for being my children. I praise God every day that He allowed me the honor of being your father. It truly is a privilege to raise you, guys. I have the greatest children on earth, and they know it. The Lord told me that my children would bring me great honor in my old age. They already have.

# Introduction:
# The Revelation of Mantles

I could not fully write on the revelation of the Josephic (meaning Joseph-like, or of Joseph) mantle until I fully unlock the revelation of mantles. As a quick reference, side-note or commentary, I will expound on the revelation of mantles—its natural and spiritual significance. This will allow the reader to better understand and have full knowledge of the meaning and operation of mantles when learning about Joseph as a whole. I want to set a foundation before revealing knowledge about Joseph.

A mantle. What is a mantle? We hear this term so many times in church, and throughout charismatic and full gospel circles. How do we define mantles? The Strong's Concordance defines a mantle as:

Mantle : [4598]—Meiyl = Meh-eel = in the sense of a covering; a robe; (i.e., upper and lower garment]: = cloke, coat, mantle, robe

[155]—addereth = ad-deh-reth = garment, glory, goodly, mantle, robe

Root word is [145]—eder -: amplitude; a mantle, splendor—goodly, robe

From these definitions above we see that a mantle can be any piece of clothing, usually worn as an upper *and* lower garment. This could be manifested in the form of a robe, which covers a person from top to bottom. ***Mantles can also be identified as a coat or cloak.*** Lastly, the Strong's Concordance describes mantles as being garments of amplitude, which means largeness or fullness. When we think of amplitude, the word amplifier comes to mind, which denotes making something loud or distinct. Words denoting amplitude would be magnitude; ampleness; fullness; glory; eminence; majesty; nobility; fame; renown; distinction. Therefore, a mantle in the Old Testament sense, speaks of a piece of clothing that shows distinction or glory. Mantles have the purpose of telling others who see it of a person's distinct ability, identity or characterization within the Kingdom of God. In modern times, and within the Full Gospel and Charismatic churches, mantles are synonymous with anointing, or ability. We see in scripture that the Bible reveals a connection between a mantle and the anointing.

> ¹[a]*BEHOLD, HOW good and how pleasant it is for brethren to dwell together in unity!* ²*It is like the precious ointment poured on the head, that ran down on the beard, even the beard of Aaron [the first high priest], <u>that came down upon the collar and skirts of his garments</u> [consecrating the whole body].* ³*It is like the dew of [lofty] Mount Hermon and the dew that comes on the hills of Zion; for there the Lord has commanded*

*the blessing, even life forevermore [upon the high and the lowly].*

                                                    Psalm 133:1-3 (Amplified)

The Bible compares the anointing of Aaron to his garment, or mantle. We also see the anointing be compared to dew that rested upon the mountains. The interpretation is that the anointing rests upon the garments, or mantle, of the one being consecrated for a certain work in the service of the Divine Creator. Therefore, Aaron, being the High Priest, was anointed for a specific purpose, and that anointing was not to touch him, but his holy garments, or mantle. In the Old Testament a special anointing oil was specifically made for the priesthood, and that anointing oil was not to touch the flesh, only the garments of the priests.

> *30And thou shalt anoint Aaron and his sons, and consecrate them, that they may minister unto me in the priest's office. 31And thou shalt speak unto the children of Israel, saying, <u>This shall be an holy anointing oil unto me throughout your generations.</u> 32<u>Upon man's flesh shall it not be poured</u>, neither shall ye make any other like it, after the composition of it: it is holy, and it shall be holy unto you.*
>
>                      Exodus 30:30-32 (King James Version - °KJV)

The anointing was made for the garment, or mantle. It was used to consecrate and activate a person for a divine use, empowering Him for a certain work.

Now that Christ has come, mantles that were once physical, such as the actual mantle of Elijah, have now become spiritual. For example, if we speak of the mantle—or anointing—of faith, we are speaking about one's distinct ability within the Kingdom to operate in the faith of God very distinctly above others. Also, if we speak of the mantle—or anointing—of wisdom, we are referring to one's ability, or gifting, to operate in prudence and discreetness so well that person clearly sticks out, and becomes distinctive from others within the Kingdom of God. It must be remembered that a mantle will always point to a person's gifting, being something God alone has set, **as a garment,** upon him/her. Therefore, when we speak of the mantle of Joseph, we are prophetically categorizing those within the Kingdom of God that operate in the same gifting and abilities of Joseph. They may not become Secretary of the Treasury of a nation like Joseph, but they operate in the same ways as Joseph- in more or less measure.

The word mantle is not used much in the Bible—only about 12 times in the KJV. It is used mostly in the story of Elijah the prophet, who wore a famous mantle, or robe, that signified his position as a major prophet of the land of Israel in his time. It wasn't until the mantle was transferred to Elisha that we are able to get a glimpse of the weight and position the mantle signified.

> *"He took up also the mantle of Elijah that fell from him, and went back, and stood by the bank of Jordan; And he took the mantle of Elijah that fell from him, and smote the waters, and said, Where is the Lord God of*

*Elijah?...And when the sons of the prophets which were to view at Jericho saw him, they said, The spirit of Elijah <u>doth</u> rest <u>on</u> Elisha. And they came to meet him, and bowed themselves to the ground before him.*"

II Kings 2:13-15

Notice, in the above scripture, when Elisha received the mantle of Elijah, the Spirit of Elijah rested upon Elisha. This "spirit" or "anointing" rested upon Elisha in much the same way as the dew rested upon the mountains of Hermon (Psalms 133:3). The mantle fell on Elisha. Elisha was now consecrated to operate in the same way that Elijah did. The mantle of Joseph acts in much the same way—it rests upon those who walk in the same principles of Joseph. Like Elisha operating in the same "spirit" of Elijah, those with the mantle of Joseph are anointed, or empowered of God, to function in the same way Joseph functioned.

## The Natural-Physical Distinction of a Mantle

Mantles carry a two-fold blessing or characteristic—physical and spiritual. The first is physical, signifying position, rank or status (i.e., the **office** of a prophet, pastor, priest, minstrel, porter, etc.). The prophets bowed before Elisha because they saw that he had the actual, physical mantle of Elijah. In other words the physical or natural representation of the mantle speaks of status or rank. In the Old Testament days, prophets wore mantles to signify their status as prophets, but these mantles varied in beauty and type in order to signify rank.

Elijah was the prophet to the nation, or "primary" prophet, and thus carried a "greater" and more "goodly" mantle than the regular prophets existing in the land at that time.

Furthermore, in those days there were "prophetic schools" where prophets went to meditate (i.e., pray) for long hours. For we know that prophetic houses existed, or we could at least speculate this, for Jezebel sought to dismantle and kill the prophets of the land, and set up a false prophetic system (I Kings 18:17-19). Thus, we can deduce that there was a community, or prophetic order, organized throughout Israel to keep the nation, and its leaders, serving the one, true God, Jehovah. We also see this in scripture when Saul became a prophet.

> "...And when they came thither to the hill, behold, a company of prophets met him; and the Spirit of God came upon him, and he prophesied among them...Therefore it became a proverb, Is Saul also among the prophets?"
>
> I Samuel 10:10,11

The "company" of prophets denote that there was some type of organized group in which these prophets came from— probably a prophetic school or spiritual order.

Set over these prophetic schools were head prophets, more akin to apostles or high-prophets. Their roles were more "administrative" in nature involving judging the land and directing other, lesser prophets, in matters of ministry and teaching, as demonstrated in the ministry of the prophet Samuel.

"Regular schools of meditation existed, led by master prophets. The master prophet, in turn, were under the leadership of primary prophets, the ones actually quoted in the bible. In these schools, people were taught meditative methods (prayer) in order to attain a closeness to God; as a side effect of such meditation, prophecy (i.e., an encounter with God such as a vision, dream or theophany) was also sometimes achieved."

*Jewish Meditation*, pg. 42

These prophets wore mantles to signify their position and rank among the prophetic houses and schools. These high-prophets, or "apostles," wore mantles of greater beauty and glory, signifying their "primary" position through the various prophetic schools. We see this in scripture with the prophet Samuel, whose prophetic apostleship moved the office and ministry of the prophetic into deeper dimensions.

*"And as Samuel turned about to go away, he (Saul) laid hold upon the skirt of his mantle, and rent it..."*

I Samuel 15:27

## The Spiritual Distinction of a Mantle

The characteristic of a mantle is spiritual, signifying an ability to move in a supernatural way (i.e., the gift of a prophet, pastor, priest, minstrel, porter, etc...), representing the type of apostolic/prophetic gifting. This gifting, in turn, allows the wearer of the mantle to operate under God's unction or power. We see this in the ministry of Elijah, who was often moved by God to perform miracles and prophetic wonders through the use of his mantle.

> *"And it was so, when Elijah heard it, that he wrapped his face in his mantle, and went out, and stood in the entering in of the cave. And, behold, there came a voice unto him, and said…"*
> I Kings 19:13 KJV

We see that the mantle initiated the voice of the Lord. How then does this great prophet need a garment to hear from the Lord? It is because the mantle represented not only his rank or position as prophetic apostleship, but his gifting or ability as well. The mantle spoke to everyone around him of his powers of prophecy and intercessory adeptness. The power of God rested not only in the man, but on his mantle also, leaving to its inheritor (Elisha) these same powers.

> *"So he departed thence, and found Elisha the son of Shaphat, who was plowing with twelve yoke of oxen before him, and he with the twelfth: and Elijah passed by him, and cast his mantle upon him. And he left his oxen, and ran after Elijah…"*
> I Kings 19:19;20 KJV

Notice, when Elijah threw his mantle upon Elisha, it spoke of a selecting of a new "primary" prophet or apostle—*a transferring of gifting*, abilities and authority. The transfer of the mantle meant a transferring of prophetic gifting. Therefore, the mantle was used for investiture or ordination into the mysteries of how to walk in the spiritual aptitudes that the mantle brought.

So then, when we speak about the mantle of Joseph, as with the mantle of Elijah, we are speaking about a transference of anointing, authority, gifting and ability. The mantle of Joseph, in the New Testament, is the power of God to operate in the same manner that Joseph operated. Will the believer have the same experiences as Joseph? Mostly likely not. Will the believer become second in command of a superpower like Ancient Egypt as Joseph? It's possible, but most likely not. The mantle of Joseph is simply the ability to move in like favor, blessing and grace as Joseph did, being gifted with the same abilities through spiritual endowment.

## The Mantle of Joseph: The Three Seasons of the Mantle

Now that we have a better understanding of mantles, it will be most convenient to explain the mantle of Joseph. Joseph's life can best be presented in three seasons, or cycles. The first season is Joseph's Pride. This is the season of his life where he receives his mantle, but with great arrogance and immaturity. At this point Joseph has been given the mantle (i.e., coat of many colors), but he doesn't have the spiritual or emotional intelligence to carry it. Therefore it results in the physical component of the mantle being stripped from him.

The second season is what I call Joseph's Humility. This is a season of Joseph's life where he goes into slavery (i.e., bondage) and the Lord uses that time to prune or teach Joseph the emotional and spiritual intelligence he needs to bear his garment—mantle. His gift was far too weighty for his age, and he needed time for his character to grow into the comparable size of his mantle. All too often, God blesses saints with great gifting, but their character is not mature enough for their mantle. Thus, they fall into mischief, resulting in a time of testing and trial (i.e., hardship) until the saint becomes obedient through the things he/she suffers. Obedience and maturity is cultivated for service.

Lastly, the third and final season of Joseph's life is his obedience. This is a season marked by victory, performance and ability to handle the mantle. He finally understands how to give glory to God instead of drawing the attention and glory to himself. Those with the Joseph mantle love self-glorification (i.e., pride), and will not come into the manifestation of what God has for them until they learn to give glory to God. The Lord restores back to Joseph the authority side of his mantle—as marked by Pharaoh putting on Joseph a royal robe (vestures), thereby replacing the coat of many colors that his brothers stripped from him (Gen. 41:42).

# 1

## Joseph's Pride

### Called, Teachable and Spoiled

It first must be known that those with the mantle of Joseph are those with a prophetic anointing, gifting and even office. If you have the mantle of Joseph, then there is a purpose for you at the end of your testing and faith. You simply have to be obedient enough to walk into it. Joseph is a type of end-time prophet to the nations. He was called of God to be a shelter to Israel.

> *"These are the generations of Jacob. Joseph, being seventeen years old, was feeding the flock with his brethren; and the lad was with the sons of Bilhah, and with the sons of Zilpah, his father's wives: and Joseph brought unto his father their evil report."*
>
> Genesis 37:2 (KJV)

Joseph, the Bible says, was "with his brethren." Joseph loved his brothers. The scriptures allude to Joseph chasing his brothers, or wanting to be around his brothers (Gen. 37:13; 16-17; Gen. 42:8). This denotes a desire for acceptance from Joseph, and a reluctance of his brothers to accept Joseph. Try to picture a younger brother who tirelessly runs after his older brothers for love and inclusion. We see this in successive chapters of scripture, when Joseph becomes governor of Egypt. The Bibles says that "Joseph knew his brothers, but they did not know him" (Genesis 42:8). Moreover, the scripture says that Joseph was separate from his brothers (Gen. 14:26). Lastly, at the end of the story of Joseph, after Jacob his father dies, his brothers worry that Joseph may try to kill them for retribution, but Joseph covers his brothers, explaining to them that he loves them and that he will support them with a lavish lifestyle in Egypt (Gen. 50:15-21). Those with the mantle of Joseph often have a difficult time being accepted by his/her "brothers" or "sisters" in the church. They can often struggle with rejection in the church. Joseph's "brothers" speak prophetically of our brothers and sisters in Christ.

The Word of God says that Joseph was specifically *with* the sons of Bilhah and Zilpah. Now, Bilhah means timidity; to palpitate; to terrify; trouble. Zilpah means to trickle; a fragrant dropping. Now Jacob had twelve sons from four different wives. Leah was the first wife, whom Jacob was tricked by Laban, her father, into marrying. Rachel was Jacob's second wife, whom Jacob worked 14 years to marry. Upon marrying both women, what I call a "sons race" began between Leah and Rachel. Both sisters, in order to win the favor of their husband, began to compete with one another by seeing who could produce the most sons, and therefore the most glory and honor. In the midst of the race, Leah employed Zilpah and Rachel employed Bilhah to become wives for Jacob in order to produce more sons. The sons of these wives speak prophetically of competition and striving—hence timidity, palpitation and trouble (Bilhah). Yet, since these sons were the sons of Jacob, on whom God placed His covenant, these sons speak of being children of worship, as well—hence fragrant dropping (Zilpah). These sons of Bilhah and Zilpah were sons of competition, striving and trouble, while simultaneously being sons of worship— sound like the church?

Now, Rachel's name means "ewe" or female sheep. Female sheep were prized as being the glory of the flock, because they had the ability to produce more sheep. The more sheep, the more prosperous the shepherd became. Also her name means "good traveler" or "to journey," denoting one who submits and follows wherever the shepherd leads. Thus, Joseph is a type of a son of submission, and the prized possession of the flock— hence Jacob's favor for Joseph. He was teachable and easily lead of the Lord, being the son of Rachel.

Those with the mantle of Joseph in the church are teachable, easily lead of God by the pastor and in agreement with the Word of God—thus God sheds His favor on them. They submit, not being stiff-necked, but they always find themselves striving with "siblings" in the church who compete for the father's (i.e., God's; pastor's; those in authority) attention. Joseph wanted acceptance from his brothers, whom in turn, denied him this access, because of his submission to his father, as well as the favor that came about as a result.

*"...and Joseph brought unto his father their evil report."*

Genesis 37:2 (KJV)

This part of the scriptures suggests that Joseph had a strong bond with his father, so much so that he was able to confide in his father the secret things of his brothers—namely their evil report. One can only speculate that this evil report moved throughout Joseph's brothers. The fact that Joseph brought their evil report to Jacob must have meant that either the evil report was against Jacob, himself, or the evil report was about the mischief that the brother's often got themselves into behind the watchful eye of their father, Jacob. Nevertheless, Joseph told on his brothers, suggesting a "suck-up" or a "tattle-tale" to authority.

All too often our churches are filled with people who speak immaturely of the pastor and the way he shepherds the flock. "They always pick Brother Biscuit to preach." "I can't stand Prophetess Pomegranate. She always keeps only Sister Sow-a-Lot as her amour bearer, and not me." "That church is funny. They always have cliques and its so hard to break into leadership." "Why does pastor want to raise money? We could be using that money to feed the poor." The sons of Bilhah and Zilpah speak of this type of Christian. Joseph, on the other hand, brought the report of this to his father. It must be remembered that Joseph was a prophet, and his mantle a prophetic one. As a result, many who have this mantle, and is close to the pastor or leader, often are able to discern those with the evil report and communicate it to their leaders. This is often done through actions, words, or even prayers. For Joseph *always* submits to authority, and therefore is given, by God, a special place of connection and fellowship with leadership. In other words, God gives him access. ✳

## The Blessing of the Coat of Many Colors

> *"Now Israel loved Joseph more than all his children, because he was the son of his old age; and he made him a coat of many colors."*
>
> Genesis 37:3 (KJV)

Jacob loved Joseph because he was the son of his old age. Joseph was the son of Rachel. What did we say about Rachel? She was submissive—easily led. She was the wife of promise for Jacob. Likewise, Joseph was the son of promise. As a result, Jacob laid favor upon Joseph, because Joseph walked in divine submission towards his father. The coat of many colors speaks of the mantle of Joseph. It was a mantle given because of favor and faithfulness—first to God, and then to authority. Jacob, being a prophet himself, transferred a blessing (an empowerment to prosper) on Joseph, in the form of a prophetic mantle. Notice, when you have favor with the those in authority over you, *God moves them to bless you* with the same blessing they have. Shortly after having the coat of many colors, Joseph begins to meet the Lord in dreams. Yet, it wasn't only a prophetic mantle, but also a blessing to move forth in prosperity. Jacob was prosperous because he served Laban for fourteen years, gaining great livestock and wealth. As a result, the inheritance and blessing of Jacob passed to Joseph in the form of the coat of many colors.

The coat of many colors was a symbolic blessing that Jacob bestowed on Joseph to both prophesy and prosper. Likewise, those with the mantle of Joseph receive the blessing to prosper and prophesy from those they serve under, namely a pastor or member of senior leadership. I say this because the blessing (the empowerment to prosper) is always passed down from one person to another through faithful service and submission. One cannot get blessed truly without first serving someone in leadership, faithfully. The bible is clear about this. In Luke 16:12 Jesus replies, "if ye have not been faithful in that which is another man's, who shall give you that which is your own?" Jacob received his own prosperity through faithful service to another man's possessions. Likewise, Joseph, as we will see, followed in his father's footsteps by being submitted and faithful to Potiphar.

When we look at Joseph's life, we see that he consistently served, even when God promoted him to be viceroy over Egypt. We have so many of what I call "rogue" pastors in leadership these days. They go out under some false unction and start a church, but no one sent them out. No one released them. They didn't serve anyone. As a consequence their churches are riddled with strife, confusion and spiritual abuse—i.e., no grace. Moreover, their churches are revolving doors. Some Sundays there are 20 members. Another Sunday, there are 13 members and two visitors. No one ever can stay planted long enough. Before long the members of these churches get offended and leave the church.

When I first came to my church, I was bouncing around the Body of Christ like a basketball. I just couldn't sit still. It was as if I couldn't fit. I'd get to one ministry and stay, but soon I'd find something wrong with the ministry and off I went to the next one. Simultaneously, I was trying to start my own ministry. Then finally one day I met my pastor who told me that I needed to be planted. "...But pastor, I'm 33 years old and I'm not in ministry, yet. Time is ticking. If I'm going to fulfill this dream, then its gotta be now! What the heck! I was baptized a minister at 17 years old. I haven't preached a sermon, yet." The man of God looked me in my eyes and said, "You're not planted, Bryan. You're here and there. You need to sit down. God is not double-minded. He isn't schizophrenic." So, I obeyed him, and I have been sitting ever since, but in this season of sitting I am learning the value of faithfulness and consistency. I'm learning not to despise small beginnings (Zechariah 4:10). The anointing of the Lord is saturating me really good, and the Lord is making the crooked places straight. You see, your pastor is a spiritual father, so he can see past your gift and into your junk. He knows you have a calling, but can you be faithful even when you are overlooked? Can you sit long enough to have that pride ministered out of you? The Lord showed me that not much got past my pastor. He is really meek, but the man can discern your junk, and you can rest assured that you are not going anywhere until you allow the Lord to deal with that crooked place. So, he tells people like me to sit, so the Lord can work the grace in us to handle the warfare that is inevitable in leadership.

I am convinced that the problem with many of these "pop-up" preachers is that they are unwilling to go through their sitting season. They are too anxious to be a wonder. Joseph's sitting season was 13 years. How long will yours be? Are you willing to go through the process? Many of us turn on The

Word Network, TBN or Daystar and we get mega-church fever. We want to go out, plant a church and buy spots on Daystar and host conferences. Good luck with that one. You must learn how to sit and savor God's grace. Serve your pastor, first lady and the leadership they ordain. Don't make a move until your pastor releases you to go out, because if you step out before the time, you are going to end up like Joseph did—in bondage because your mantle was too big for your character.

> *"And when his brethren saw that their father loved him more than all his brethren, they hated him, and could not speak peaceably to him."*
>
> Genesis 37:4 (KJV)

Man-o-man, if I had a dollar for every time my haters spoke a word of ill-will against me, then I would have a nice little "grip" to place into the offering bucket. Haters (i.e., your enemies) will snuffle and snarl at your blessing. They will hate on you because they see where you are going. Joseph's brothers saw the coat, for it is written, "...when his brethren **saw** that their father loved him more..." Notice, in scripture we read that Jacob loved Joseph, so he made Joseph a coat.

> *"Now Israel loved Joseph more than all his children, because he was the son of his old age; and* he made him a coat of many colors.*"*
>
> Genesis 37:3 (KJV)

There was a connection between Jacob's love for Joseph and the coat. Now remember, Joseph received a blessing from Jacob. This blessing was both a prophetic blessing and a blessing of prosperity. It spoke of Joseph's inheritance. His future blessing. When he wore the coat, it spoke of a time coming that he would have a greater inheritance than his brothers. When we study scripture we find that the Tribe of Joseph was broken up into two tribes, Ephraim and Manasseh. Further study reveals that these two tribes were given the biggest inheritance, or portion of land, when the Israelites finally conquered the promised land. This blessing was reserved for the firstborn, but Reuben forfeited his blessing when he uncovered his father's nakedness by sleeping with Bilhah, one of his father's concubines. Therefore, the blessing passed to Joseph. It must also be remembered that Joshua, successor to Moses, was of the tribe of Joseph (Manasseh & Ephraim combined). He led the children of Israel into their promised land—the inheritance.

Those with the mantle of Joseph have a special gifting to walk close with God. This, in turn, causes a glory to be on them for peculiarity and distinction. The coat of many colors was peculiar. It was different. As a result, there was something on Joseph that spoke of future blessings. Likewise, those with the mantle of Joseph have an anointing of distinction on them in their sitting season, which is a season of their life when they have not been released into their destiny. Yet, they are marked by the presence of God in a peculiar way. This favor is so strong that their enemies can see that the Lord, and those in authority, have favored them. Joseph's brothers saw his future by seeing the coat of many colors, and thus realized that their father (symbolic of a person in authority—or God) loved him. Many times those with the mantle of Joseph have favor with people in authority, and God, so much so that these people of authority bless them in secret through prayer, resulting in an anointing of glory in their lives so strong that it is noticed by others.

> *"But he that is greatest amoung you shall be your servant. And whosoever shall exalt himself shall be abased; and he that shall humble himself shall be exalted."*
>
> Matthew 23:11-12

Your coat of many colors, or anointing, tells everyone around you that God is going to use you mightily, but since it offends others and suggests that you are going to be a great one in the Kingdom, the Lord moves you into places of lowliness to keep you humble. You will not be asked to be on the leadership team, you will be asked to serve in parking lot ministry. You will be relied upon to vacuum. The most humbling thing about it is that the Lord will personally see to it that you have a strong grace for it. So, as you are cleaning crap up off the toilets, God is giving you prophetic words about the next move of God, and what direction He is about to move the church. The Lord is speaking into your spirit the same Word your pastor is giving on Sunday—a day before the sermon is preached. In other words, as you serve, intentionally, you are moving in unison with the House.

## Josephs Are Prophets: Called to be Stewards of Revelation

> *"And Joseph dreamed a dream, and he told it his brethren: and they hated him yet the more. And he said unto them, Hear, I pray you, this dream which I have dreamed: For, behold, we were binding sheaves in the field, and lo, my sheaf arose, and also stood upright; and, behold, your sheaves stood round about, and made obeisance to my sheaf. And his brethren said to him, Shalt thou indeed reign over us? Or shalt thou indeed have dominion over us? And they hated him yet the more for his dreams, <u>and for his words</u>. And he dreamed yet another dream, and told it his brethren, and said, Behold, I have dreamed a dream more; and , behold, the sun and the moon and the eleven stars made obeisance to me. And he told it to his father, and it to his brethren: and his father rebuked him, and said unto him, What is this dream that thou hast dreamed? Shall I and thy mother and thy brethren indeed come to bow down ourselves to thee to the earth? And his brethren envied him; but his father observed the saying."*
>
> Genesis 37:5-11(KJV)

Joseph made the mistake of telling his dream to his brothers. Remember, the mantle of Joseph is a prophetic mantle. Also, it must be understood that shortly after Joseph received the coat of many colors, he began to meet God in dreams. God began disclosing secrets to him. The problem was that he was not mature enough to use his gifts of revelation in a proper way. His mantle (i.e., coat of many colors) was too big for his character. Joseph was not mature enough to keep his revelations to himself. The Bible says that:

> *"He that keepeth his mouth keepeth his life: but he that openeth wide his lips shall have destruction."*
>
> Proverbs 13:3

Never enter any type of Christian group, circle or congregation disclosing revelations unless proper authority has released you to do it. If you do, you will draw warfare to yourself. One of the most dangerous giftings in the Body of Christ is the prophetic gifting. This is because it is a doorway or gate to heaven, and when the Lord begins speaking with you it says to others that God has made you special, even over them. The Apostle Paul warned against speaking too much about what God shows you in the book of Corinthians.

> *"It is not expedient for me doubtless to glory. I will come to visions and revelations of the Lord... For though I would desire to glory, I shall not be a fool; for I will say the truth: but now I forbear, lest any man should think of me above that which he seeth me to be, or that he heareth of me. And lest I should be exalted above measure through the abundance of the revelations, there*

*was given to me a thorn in the flesh, the messen-*
*ger of Satan to buffet me, lest I should be exalted*
*above measure. "*

II Corinthians 12:1;6-7

Paul was saying that he loves to glory, or talk about the abundance of revelations that God gives him. Yet, he said that he will not be a fool. In essence, he was saying that it is not good for a man to disclose the personal revelations of God, because then men would exalt him above that which God made him to be. In other words, man would begin giving glory to himself, as opposed to God. This was the mistake Joseph made to his brethren. If a man exalts himself, he will be humbled.

It must be remembered that the Apostle Paul wrote most of the New Testament, receiving it by revelation. God spoke to him so much that the scripture says that he was literally taken up into heaven to see paradise and hear wonderful, heavenly words too pure to be spoken. Yet despite all of this, he became wise through his sufferings and concluded that he will not glory in the revelatory disclosing of heaven that the Lord was giving him. He came to this conclusion, because Satan humbled him, keeping his flesh under subjection through trial and testing. In other words, he learned by experience that speaking about revelations and visions to others had an element of self-exaltation, and when he did this, the Lord cut him down.

Joseph made the mistake of telling his brothers this vision in order to exalt himself. For, he already knew that his brothers hated him for the coat's sake. Why in the world would he add insult to injury by disclosing that not only the Lord gave him a dream, but in the dream he was going to be exalted over his brethren? I suspect Joseph did this as an act of self-glorification and retaliation. I'm sure they ostracized him because he was given a coat of many colors. I'm sure they mocked him and made him the butt of many jokes, being the younger sibling. When he had the dream, he became proud, in turn mocking his brothers for their envy. Yet, the revealing of the dream to his brothers tells us that Joseph wasn't ready for exaltation, but humiliation, because he exalted himself and not God by telling his brothers the dream.

When the Lord begins opening heaven up to you, then it is at that time to become wise with the information being given to you. Many people will take your revelation as code for, "I will some day be exalted over you," or "I'm better than you, because God allows me to walk in a higher prophetic dimension than you do." They will automatically locate the spirit of pride in you, and plot, through prayer and sedition, to destroy your future and vision. Those with the mantle of Joseph will have to take a very extra precaution so as not to exalt themselves in this way. The anointing that goes along with the mantle of Joseph includes strong powers of visions, dreams and revelations—the understanding of dark sayings, parables and riddles. These encounters will be so exciting and insightful it will be hard to keep it locked in your heart. There will be other times, when the Lord will release you to share divine information about important events and people. You must be very careful. The Lord will give you information to test your maturity with it. As for Joseph, he flaunted his gifting before his brothers, and paid a heavy price, proving that his character was too small for his mantle.

*"Let a man so account of us, as of the ministers of Christ, and stewards of the mysteries of God. Moreover it is required in stewards, that a man be found faithful. "*

I Corinthians 4:1-2 (KJV)

Since the mantle of Joseph is a prophetic mantle, it is the duties of those blessed with it to keep the mysteries of God, faithfully. What do I mean? The gifting of the prophetic is very essential to the end-time church right now, because Satan moves by deception. As a result, it takes the anointing of the SEER to understand what is being done in the dark. Therefore, the Lord needs faithful prophets to keep, manage, curate, protect, guard, audit, treasure and safeguard the mysteries, or secrets, of God. He needs men and women who will write down what they see and lay up the visions for an appointed time. In these last days it is God's desire for the prophetic dimension to be manifested in a librarian-type fashion. Librarians are keepers of knowledge. They lay up knowledge. They do a great deal of categorizing and organizational administration in order to keep books and knowledge in safety for an appointed time. They protect books and knowledge from harm, or from being lost, damaged or stolen. So likewise, the Lord is raising up end-time Josephs to be keepers and stewards of the revelation, knowledge and artfulness of God. We are in a season of divine understanding. The Lord is disclosing the mysteries of heaven and witty inventions. We are in a season of divine cunning and clever works. Understanding and knowledge is increasing in the earth realm. This is seen by the sudden boom in technology—which is man's understanding of heavenly concepts.

God is ministering to his prophets divine genius and skilful cunning to advance the Kingdom of God THROUGH REVELA-TION, but it takes wisdom and faithfulness of His mysteries. We see this in scripture where the prophet Daniel is told by angels to lay up revelation and keep it.

> *"Hitherto is the end of the matter. As for me Daniel, my cogitations much troubled me, and my countenance changed in me: but I kept the matter in my heart."*
>
> Daniel 7:28

> *"...But thou, O Daniel, shut up the words and seal the book, even to the time of the end: many shall run to and fro, and knowledge shall be increased."*
>
> Daniel 12:4

We must not take this charge lightly. For those blessed with the mantle of Joseph are those charged and required of God to be stewards—faithful stewards—of the mysteries (dark sayings, riddles and parables) of God.

## Josephs Must Use Discretion When Disclosing Revelation

As a prophet in training there will be times that you will miss the mark. You will pay for it, but don't worry, its just God teaching you and pruning you how to use His gifting. I remember being about 17 years old, and the Lord gave me a prophetic word about a minister's son. I knew it was from the Lord, but I found out quickly that it was not for me to disclose. I had the Word in my belly, and I was still immature in the prophetic things of God, so I wrote the minister, telling him what thus saith the Lord. He spoke with me about it, saying that I was accurate and right on. There was no change in the minister, outwardly. Life just continued on as normal. Then, the Lord gave me a dream. In the dream I got up in church to minister to a group of teens, and I did an excellent job. Then, my pastor came up to the pulpit and took the microphone from my hand and said, "Can I teach, now?" As he began to address the group I saw that he had incurred a wound on his neck. It was bandaged in white gauze. The Lord quickly revealed to me that I had wounded him. I felt so foolish, because I didn't want to hurt him. I loved him. I then had another dream in which we both were walking down a flight of stairs and I began to stumble, while he walked down without stumbling. The Lord was showing me that he was much more mature in the Word than I was, and that he knew what he needed to do with his son. Again, I felt foolish. Sometimes the Lord will show you things for the sake of prayer, not disclosure, and when you fail to handle His revelations in a mature way, then you will be humbled.

There will be other times when the Lord will lead you to disclose information. A few years ago I had a dream involving a pastor. I inquired of God as whether or not I should disclose it to the man of God, and I got a release to do so. In the dream, me and a prominent pastor in the city was sitting in the overflow section while this pastor ministered to his congregation. The prominent pastor kept raising his hand to interrupt the service. He wanted to give this pastor some wisdom about the direction of the church. This pastor, moved in pride and ignored the prominent pastor. You could tell that he was annoyed that the prominent pastor was interrupting the service. He was upset this man was telling him how to grow his church, even though the prominent pastor had a huge congregation with much more exposure, nationally and internationally. The prominent pastor raised his hand two more times, but got rebuked by the other pastor. Finally the prominent pastor got up and literally stopped the service and told the other pastor to come outside. Once the stubborn pastor humbled himself enough to obey, cars from everywhere entered into the parking lot to attend the church. The interpretation of the dream was saying that there were prophets, or men of wisdom, set in the church aside from the regular congregation, who had understanding and counsel to assist the pastor in the problems he was facing. Yet in order to get the wisdom the pastor was going to have to submit and realize that he didn't have all the answers. Needless to say, this was hard to do for him. He was a stubborn man. At the time of the dream, we were having problems with membership. I told the dream to this pastor, but shortly after I told him the dream his attitude changed towards me. He wouldn't speak with me anymore. I couldn't get in to his council. He wouldn't return my phone calls. Then, about three months later, the prominent pastor, who was in my dream, planted another church exactly next door to our church. His church was filled to capacity every Sunday, but ours contained barely 30 active members.

The pastor's pride wouldn't heed the prophetic word God was trying to get to him. If he would have heeded the wisdom God was trying to give him, then more than likely his church would still be in operation, today. Needless to say, the church had to close due to lack of membership, and the pastor gave what remained of his congregation to the prominent pastor. When the Lord directs you to do something, then He will back you up with signs following.

Lastly, there will be times when God will tell you to sit on a revelation. I remember one time I was sitting on the couch watching a movie and the Lord began to speak to me about a particular man of God. I jumped up and began writing the revelation down. I was excited for the man of God, as God was about to seriously exalt him. So naturally I wanted to share the revelation with him, discreetly. Before I did, I asked God to show me if this was something He wanted me to disclose to him. Sure enough, that night, I fell asleep and had a dream. In the dream I had a prophetic word for a very prominent evangelist. I approached her, asking her if I could give her a word. She refused. I realized at that time that I had the gifting, but not the office of a prophet, and therefore had basically no real authentication—in her eyes. God showed me that the Word I had for the man of God would be treated in much the same way. Needless to say, I kept the revelation a secret, and avoided falling out of favor with a man of God that was divinely appointed to my life. The Bible says to acknowledge God in all your ways that He may direct your path (Proverbs 3:6). This is especially true when deciding whether or not to just give revelations that God "shows" you. Remember to inquire of the Lord before giving words of Prophecy. Get a release, or "Green

Light," in your spirit before proceeding. Many times it's not your gift that men refuse, it's how they perceive you.

Weeks later the Lord came to me saying, "Bryan, in this season of your life I want you to work, not prophesy." Needless to say, I kept my mouth closed about the Word **I wanted** to give to the man of God, and focused on work. Weeks later, a very accurate prophetess came to the church and prophesied the same Word God gave me about the man of God almost word for word—in an even greater way. Many times the Lord will give revelations and understanding not for the purposes of telling everybody, but for the purposes of being your friend—entrusting you with His Word. True friends keep secrets. Surely, the Lord will do nothing but reveal His secrets to His servants the prophets. Prophets are friends of God. If I gave that word to the man of God, he wouldn't have taken it as seriously. He wouldn't have etched it on his heart.

Joseph, being young and immature, didn't realize his transgression. He moved in self-glorification, telling his revelation of exaltation to an already jealous people. The result was disastrous. Whenever we move in pride and self-focus with the gifting that God gives us, then it becomes clear to heaven that we do not have the character for the mantle. God then begins to orchestrate and mobilize events and people with the authority to strip us of our mantle. As with Joseph, we see that he moved out in ministry too soon. He allowed his mantle to puff him up in pride. Those with the mantle of Joseph must be cautious so as to not move in pride because of the great revelation and performance the mantle brings. It is required of you to be humble, or you will lose what God has given you through strife.

*"And when they saw him afar off, even before he came near unto them, they <u>conspired</u> against him to slay him.*

Genesis 37:18

The mantle of Joseph is a mantle that brings warfare against you through conspiracy. Taken from the Webster's dictionary, the word conspire means "to join in secret agreement to do an unlawful or wrongful act." If you are to carry the mantle of Joseph, then you have to be one who can move skillfully against conspiracy. You must be able to see it coming, and move prudently to dismantle it. This requires wisdom. Your enemies will always have a secret plan against you, and it takes the wisdom and subtlety of God to out-maneuver those that seek to stop the call of God on your life. I believe strongly that conspiracy is a snare that follows those with a great call on their life. As with the mantle of Joseph, get used to people plotting to hijack and diffuse the glory of God on your life. Conspiracy among brethren is usually birthed out of envy. The Bible says that Joseph's brothers envied him (Gen. 37:11). The Bible also says that Joseph's enemies "sorely grieved him, and shot at him, and hated him" (Genesis 49:23). Those that envy you will conspire against you in order to make you fall. If you are one that carries this mantle, then prepare to fight battles that are undercover. Learn to defend yourself against secret wars, plots and plans. Those that are gifted in sedition and sabotage will come at you, but this is the plan of God so that you will stay humble. Joseph was constantly whipped (grieved and shot at) so that he was kept humble.

# 2

## Joseph's Humility

### Oh God, Here Comes That King

*"And they said one to another, Behold, this dreamer cometh."*

Genesis 37:19

Ah, how famous are these words. Whenever you have a dream in your heart, and you possess the mantle and gifting of Joseph, the people around you, especially those brothers and sisters in the church that secretly envy you, will mutter these words in their hearts. They will say in themselves, "Here comes the know-it-all," or "Here comes Mr. Prophet, the great super revelator." They do this because at this stage in your life you are not bearing the fruit of the dream. They also say it because they just plain hate you. I can't tell you how many times folks have mistaken my hunger and zeal for God as pride and arrogance. For Joseph, his coat represented a child prodigy of the anointing—a young, spoiled genius in the things of the Spirit.

As a result of his gifting, he flaunted it a bit, immaturely. Yet, the dreams represented a zeal for God. His insight into the supernatural realm was so interesting that he just had to tell his brothers. He paid dearly for being so naïve. When you are gifted and immature often people will hate on you for the anointing and dream God has given you. It must be remembered that every time  you come around, those people that can't stand your calling will always say in their hearts, "here comes the dreamer; the one with the big plans. Here comes the one that says he is going to be king, someday."

## Josephs Must Contend With Humility

> *"And it came to pass, when Joseph was come unto his brethren, that they stript Joseph out of his coat, his coat of many colours that was on him. And they took him, and cast him into a pit... And they sat down to eat bread."*
>
> Genesis 37:23-25

I think the above scripture is the most interesting of the whole Joseph story. The very thing the brothers envied was the thing God allowed them to take. In other words, the Lord allowed the brothers to see Joseph fall. The most interesting thing about this is that the scripture says that they sat down to bread. What does this say? This says that they were so unconcerned and happy that Joseph was out of the way that they rejoiced and broke bread. They ate. Wow! Ever had a so-called brother hate you so much that they do all they can to get you out of a position, and rejoice when you are out? The Mantle of

Joseph carried with it envy and hate—strife. People will not like you for no reason. They will plot to uproot you and make your life miserable. The most extraordinary thing about this is that it was Joseph's brothers who did this. In other words, it is your brothers and sisters in the church that you will find the most warfare from.

God allowed Joseph's brothers to humiliate him by taking the thing that symbolized his prophetic position in God. I mentioned earlier that soon after Jacob gave Joseph his coat, God began to meet Joseph in dreams. Thus, there was a connection between the coat of many colors and the gift of prophecy and revelation—like Elijah and his mantle. Notice, when you have the mantle of Joseph, and your character is not big enough for the mantle/coat, then God will allow those that envy you to strip it from you. The coat speaks of the anointing, or the thing that God puts on you that makes you great. When you flow in pride, then the Lord will give you over to the desires of your enemies, not to kill you, but to humble you and purify you of your pride so that you can once again wear the mantle. Joseph was in leadership at an early age, for his father sent him to oversee the business of his brothers (Genesis 37:13). Yet, he was too immature for his position, not because he was incompetent, but because he flaunted his position by giving his father the evil report of his brothers (Genesis 37:3), as well as acting as if one day his brothers would serve him (Genesis 37:10).

Those with the mantle of Joseph tend to draw too much confidence from their gifts instead of from the one who created the gift and placed it inside them. There is a danger of having confidence in yourself as opposed to God. This confidence is called pride. When we are prideful, and loved by God

41

simultaneously, the Lord is obligated to chastise and prune us. When we flaunt our gifting and abilities before others, we open ourselves up for attacks of darkness and closed doors of opportunity. Although we are faithful to God, we can often become prideful before our enemies. When this happens, the Lord will cause our enemies to strip us of the very anointing that made us great by setting up snares that cause us to fall. We see this in Joseph's brothers who conspired against him and "cast him into a pit." As soon as the coat was stripped off Joseph, he was cast into a pit. It was almost as if the authority to save himself fell away with the coat. The Lord exalted his enemies to purify him of pride so that he could fulfill his destiny. Those with the mantle of Joseph will always find that God will exalt their enemies in order to refine their character.

## God Will Exalt Our Enemies to Mature Our Character

I used to always complain because the Lord would constantly exalt my enemies. I hated it. The very ones who moved and operated in witchcraft, manipulating those in the church, were the very ones whom God used to humble me. Here I am living right, trying to obey my pastor and blessing the church, but God exalts some manipulative, enemy who calls himself my brother or sister in Christ. Or, at least that was my perspective. God loves them, too. The real story was that somewhere along the line I failed to give honor, or humble myself, to these same brothers and sisters, and the Lord humbled me by exalting them. Has that ever happened to you? Well, if you have the mantle of Joseph, get used to it. God will deliberately put you in a pit, and make your anointing of no effect until you learn the sweet fragrance of humility.

> *"Rejoice not when thine enemy falleth, and let not thine heart be glad when he stumbleth: Lest the Lord see it, and it displease him, and he turn away his wrath from him"*
>
> Proverbs 24:17-18

God will never give you land you are unable to occupy. If you cannot handle the position or mantle that God has given you, then prepare for demotion. When I first started attending my church, I was so eager to become a part of the leadership team on staff. I thought I finally found the right church. I was well liked, and it was easy to love everyone. I had a great relationship with my pastor, as well as those on the leadership staff. I attended church regularly. I fasted and prayed. I gave generously to the church. I had the outward appearance of a leader, but God was more concerned with my inward chaos. I knew I wasn't ready, but the gifting in me was fully matured. My character was not. I became frustrated with myself, and it showed up in my attitude towards my pastor and those around me. So, I inquired of the Lord, and he gave me a dream. In the dream I had two brand new, white cars in my driveway fresh off the lot. I was overjoyed to have these cars. One was a convertible, Ford Mustang and the other was a Chevy Impala, rag top. My two sons got in the Impala and put the car in reverse, backing out the driveway. The only problem was that Jeremiah was 9 years old, and Josiah was 5. Needless to say, they were too young **and immature**, to drive the car.

My father was with me, and he managed to get them to stop the vehicle in the middle of the street. My oldest son, Joshua, backed the Mustang out too, but the speed and muscle of the car was too much for him to control and he backed right into the Impala that was in the middle of the street. Despite me trying to direct him not to drive the car, my heart sank as I watched the cars being damaged. My sons were fine, thank God, but the cars had extensive damage.

I woke from the dream and immediately knew what the Lord was communicating to me. First, the two white cars spoke of ministry. I wanted to be in ministry so bad that it was all I thought about. It was almost an obsession. I was fanatical about it. My sons spoke of immaturity. My father and I spoke of maturity, or spiritual authority trying to teach or lead the sons down the correct path. We warned them not to enter the car yet, because they were too young and immature to drive such advanced pieces of machinery. Once they started operating the cars against our wills, they then crashed the machinery. This was God confirming to me that I was too immature to operate in ministry at that time in my life. Joshua was going on 14 at the time of my dream. In two years he would be at the required age of maturity to begin learning how to operate a car. Likewise, the Lord was communicating to me that I needed to sit under the Word for a season, maturing in the Lord, and then I would be eligible, or "old enough," to begin **training** for ministry. If I launched out, despite the direction of my spiritual authorities, I would damage my ministry beyond repair. Secondly, the two, white cars represented a double portion. This double portion required seasons of submission and preparation. I desperately wanted the same anointing as my pastor, but it was going to take obedience and seasons of obscurity.

All too often we desire to move into positions beyond the scope of our character. Joseph possessed a mantle his character was not ready for. He needed to learn humility by way of service. It must be remembered that Joseph served his father. Joseph, and his willingness to serve, speaks of a gifting in the ministry of helps. We will see that Joseph spent a great portion of his life serving. Why? Because the Lord was refining his character and getting him ready for a greater season in his life. Joseph was like Jesus. He was about his father, Jacob's, business. Joseph served spiritual authority loyally, but the place of leadership that he was in was something his character could not handle. With Jacob, he obtained his mantle by way of favor, not hard work and perseverance. God had to bring him into a place where he could learn faithfulness.

## Josephs Are Matured Through Bondage

*"Come, and let us sell him to the Ishmeelites...
And the Midianites sold him into Egypt unto
Potiphar, an officer of Pharaoh's, and captain of
the guard."*

Genesis 37:27;36

Joseph's brothers sold him into slavery. Slavery speaks of bondage; servitude; hard times. Notice, Joseph was under the comforts of his father. He enjoyed a position of leadership and management under his father in that he didn't have to be out in the hot desert with his brothers tending the sheep. He was spoiled. He enjoyed a coat of many colors, which speaks of prosperity and ease. Have you ever enjoyed the blessings of God when others had to struggle?

As an only child, my mother emphasized the importance of education. She received her undergraduate and Master's degrees in education, and then went on to get her law degree. Due to hard work and connections, my mother became well known in the city, and I found myself mingling with millionaires, mayors and political leaders. An aristocratic spirit had been ministered into me. She prided herself on knowledge and understanding, dedicating her life to fighting racism and injustice. In retrospect, I think this attributed to the prophetic call on my life, for injustice grieves those who flow in the prophetic. We attended the African Methodist Episcopal Church (A.M.E.). This was the first formal, official African-American church in America—very traditional.

My childhood was full of fond memories of bar association meetings, award ceremonies and exclusive dinners honoring the intellectually erudite. I was taught proper etiquette, and became articulate and witty at an early age. The Bible says that knowledge puffs up, or makes proud, but love edifies (I Cor 8:1). After high school, I married and moved out of my hometown to attend college. I attended school full time, managed a family of five and worked full time—successfully. After graduating from college with a degree in corporate finance, I worked for a local company as an accountant. Because of hard work and favor from my superiors, I found myself getting promoted every two years, which enabled me to live very comfortably. Within three years after graduating college, I found myself assisting in the management of the organization's enormous

$200 million portfolio as an investment analyst. I was on my way. I knew it, and my bosses knew it. In two years I was going to be Treasury Manager. In ten, I was going to be CFO. Yet, I wanted to pursue ministry so bad, I dreamt about it every day.

My job "status" caused me to look down on people with less "education" than me. I wore suits to work. I ate dinner with VP's. I'd have meetings with the CEO. I would tell my wife not to spend time with certain "friends" because they "weren't going where we were going." My family members all liked being around me, but at the same time they envied my "refined," "bourgeoisie" perspective. I knew many of them envied my wife and I, and wanted to see us lose what little we had built up. There were people in my family who didn't like the fact that my wife and I were married, and often prophesied our demise and divorce. I shrugged it off as if they were mad, and kept on moving. At times, I found myself judging those who had less of an "intellectual" outlook as I did, or those who did not share the same moral outlook as me. In essence, like Joseph, I was saying to those in my family, "one day I will rule over you. I'm higher than you. I'm more blessed." I knew that these people hated me, because they could not speak peaceably to me. Yet, they were Christians, and I knew that they had conversations to God about my arrogance.

My steady advancement and knowledge found its humbling when I was fired for reasons beyond my doing. My life quickly went into a tailspin, and I found myself on welfare (something I told myself I would never do), living with parents and unable to get back on the horse—financially. Needless to say, the Lord was humbling me through my enemies, even the enemies in my own family who were very jealous of my perceived "success." When I lost my job it seemed many trials began hitting my life all at once. Family members close to me got in trouble with the law. Bills piled sky high. Lights got shut off. Heat got turned off. I struggled with anxiety and depression. I kept losing more jobs. I went through a great deal of humbling, but the Lord began working a precious character in me that is bringing me to greater greats and higher heights. Like Joseph, I was sold into slavery (bondage) to refine my character and learn humility in order to fill the mantle properly.

Slavery speaks of hard bondage. In essence, slavery can depict times when God allows hard situations to come upon you; times when you are commanded by God to serve under, not to rule over; times when defeat takes hold of you, and you no longer find the overcoming spirit you once had to fight the dark situation you are in. Lack is a fruit of slavery. Strife is a fruit of slavery. Bitterness is also a fruit of slavery. It is at these times that you find yourself at odds with self, being required of God to face self, while having to motivate self to overcome self. When all this happens, it is a time to submit to the process of God and allow Him to work character in you. Joseph was given to Potiphar as a slave. This speaks of no longer being able to work in a capacity of leadership, but in a capacity of servitude. The experience of slavery was just what Joseph needed to get the comfort of being the "favored one" out of him, and the character of being the "dreamer" in him. He was taken out of the place where his gift was celebrated and put in the place where his character would be developed. He was being trained for his dream, and didn't even know it. Your dark seasons are times of training for the season God requires you to reflect His Glory.

## God Brings You Down, So that You Will God-Up

*"...And Joseph was brought down to Egypt."*
Genesis 39:1

When I studied the story of Joseph, I thought this passage of scripture was particularly distinctive. It stood out to me. The Bible says that Joseph was brought down. I feel that this speaks prophetically of his humbling. Joseph was brought down, because his brothers, the ones he thought loved him, conspired against him to humble him. They succeeded. There will always be a time when the Lord will bring you down. Prepare for it, because its coming. In order to live in this world, we will have to battle the spirit of pride, and when we cannot fight this demon effectively, then the Lord steps in to bring us down. Notice, Joseph was brought down to Egypt. He was brought down by being sent into a strange place, a place of the world. Egypt speaks of worldliness and carnality. Before, he only dealt with his father's sons, but now he must deal with the world. In other words, all Joseph was used to dealing with was the comforts of his father's house. Jacob was rich (Genesis 32:13-16). Thus, Joseph was used to getting what he wanted, when he wanted it. He served his father, but he also lived a privileged life. He didn't know hard bondage. He didn't know the "grit" of the world. He didn't know what life was like to have to fend for himself. He was taken from a place of security and placed into a place of insecurity and strangeness. It was time for him to learn what life was like without the support of his comfortable place—Jacob's house. How many times has God taken you from a place of comfort, and placed you into a tight place?

> *"The steps of a good man are ordered by the Lord: and he delighteth in his way. Though he fall, he shall not be utterly cast down: for the Lord upholdeth him with his hand."*
>
> Psalms 37:23-24

Those with the mantle of Joseph will be placed into a tight place to be tested of God for a season. I call this the sitting season. The sitting season is a place of lowness. It is the place between the prophetic Word and the promise coming to pass. It is a season of preparation and learning. When you sit, you are shorter, or at a lower position, than when you stand. I derived the term from when a pastor sits a leader down so that the leader cannot operate in his/her gift. This is often true of worship leaders who sin, and the pastor is forced to "sit" them down. The sitting season requires rejuvenation and renewal. It requires that, like the worship leader, you swallow your pride and deactivate your gift to build character. You are now in a place outside your comfort zone, and required to be patient until God (i.e., the pastor) calls you back to a place of reinstatement. How you sit determines how you stand. As for Joseph, he was now commanded of God to sit, being taken out of his comfort zone and thrust into a place of testing. This path for us could be God taking away money; going through an embarrassment; or anything that God uses to get our attention in order for us to depend on Him. It is now Joseph's turn to see how the "street" people live. He now can't warm himself by Jacob's fire. He can't where nice clothes. He has to wear the clothes of a slave. He now has no money. He is talked about and treated poorly. The sitting season could be a season of lack, or tightness. It is a season in which God deliberately cuts away things in your life so that you are not trying to get the "big" before you know how to manage the "small." The sitting season is a place that is prophetic. It is a place in your life that communicates to you the need to be responsible, forcing you to go to God for instruction and help.

## Josephs Are Gifted Servants

*And Joseph found grace in his sight, <u>and he served him:</u>*

Genesis 39:4

Joseph was a servant. Notice, when you serve, you find grace in the sight of your leaders, or those whom you serve under. People with the mantle of Joseph are anointed in the ministry of helps. They are gifted in serving. They love lowliness; they condescend to men of low estate (Romans 12:16). In other words, they like hanging around servants, or people of low reputation, while at the same time being of noble birth or spirit. We have entered into a time when the church puts emphasis on leadership. The American church is surrounded by the American ideology of corporatism, globalism and imperialism. Our society teaches us that we have to be the best. It teaches us that leadership is being a senior pastor, CEO or successful businessman. I believe that this is false leadership. True leadership is service. Everyone in the church knows this, but many seldom embrace it. Everyone wants to preach, but no one wants to serve. As I grow older and wiser about ministry, and what it entails behind the scenes, I realize that preaching or teaching the Word of God is a bonus to ministry. Its something God throws in the mix to make the work of the ministry fun. The real work of ministry is making sure the needs of God's people are met. It is visiting the sick and shut in. It is giving money to the poor; helping people on drugs; counseling families attacked with divorce; cleaning the church.

> *"..But he that is greatest amoung you shall be your servant."*
>
> Matthew 23:11

The word great in the Greek means to be larger; elder; greater(est); big; high; large; loud; mighty; strong. In other words, those who want to be highest, larger, loudest and stronger must be those that excel at serving. The word servant is the Greek word *Diakoneo*, which is where we get the root word for deacon or deaconess. This word literally means to be an attendant; to wait upon others. It literally means to wait upon others as a host, friend or teacher. Furthermore, the word means to administer or minister; serve; literally to run errands; to administer; minister; ministering; ministration. Another word for serving literally means to be a waiter; a teacher; a pastor. In order to be a minister one literally has to be in attendance. If you have dreams of being a banking executive, then you can't call off of work 5 times a year. You have to be in attendance. If you want to be a business owner, you can't neglect your business. If you want to be a successful student, then you have to be in attendance in class. You have to be in attendance at the library. You must attend to those books!

Joseph excelled at serving, because he made a decision to serve. He realized his own pride. He saw his own pride at the hands of his brothers, and lowered himself to those in authority over him. The Bible says that he "served" Potiphar (Genesis 39:4). Why would the Bible bring this out? Joseph had to serve, being a slave, right? He had no other choice. Yet, the Bible accentuates that Joseph SERVED Potiphar. In other words, Joseph made a conscious decision to serve; to lower himself; to attend to Potiphar and all that his master had; to love Potiphar; to have a servant's heart and attitude. Notice, whenever you truly serve, you will have to suffer, at some point, at the hands of injustice. Your masters (i.e., bosses or those in authority over you) will hurt you. They will rebuke you. They will overlook you. They will wound you, because they are human. Do you treat them with a bad attitude, or do you serve?

## The Blessings of the Mantle

> *"And it came to pass from the time that he had made him overseer in his house, and over all that he had, that the Lord BLESSED the Egyptian's house for Joseph's sake; and the BLESSING of the Lord was upon all that he had in the house, and in the field. "*
>
> Genesis 39:5

The blessing came upon Potiphar, because Joseph was faithful to serve. Now, we see a connection between the blessing of God and faithfulness. The defining and outstanding trait of the mantle of Joseph is gifting and faithfulness. Faithfulness, or diligence, is something that is learned over time. It is not something that is inherent in the mantle of Joseph, but it is something that is obtained through having the mantle. The mantle, itself, moves you prophetically into position that requires you to learn faithfulness. God does this, because it is something that God has to minister into you for where you are going. This scripture is interesting in that it tells the reader that this blessing came over time. The scripture reads, "And it came to pass..." Therefore, there was a season in between the time Joseph was made a slave in Potiphar's house and overseer of his house. Responsibility comes by measure, and if you are called to bear the burden of the mantle of Joseph, then you are going to have to learn patience. It is required of you to stay in the place that God has divinely positioned you, so that you are able to learn that position fully. Then, when promotion comes, the Lord will move you up to another position. I believe in my heart that promotion comes based on your level of faithfulness at each level. You are going to have to learn how to humble yourself for the mantle. The mantle requires seasons of learning. Faithfulness does not come over night. I've always thought that Joseph was just faithful. No. He learned it over time. He grew in it. As a result, the Lord caused him to be promoted. The mark of the mantle of Joseph is promotion. Wherever Joseph went, he was promoted.

> *"And the Lord was with Joseph, and he was a prosperous man; and he was in the house of his master the Egyptian. And his master saw that*

*the Lord was with him, and that the Lord made
all that he did to prosper in his hand. And Joseph found grace in his sight, and he served him:
and he made him overseer over his house, and
all that he had he put into his hand."*

Genesis 39:2-4

One of the first things we see Joseph doing is prospering in
his slavery. Joseph prospered because the Lord was with him.
The Lord was ministering in and through him. He found grace
in the sight of God and man. Notice, those with the mantle of
Joseph have the Lord with them. This is the defining factor of
anyone with any type of mantle. When the Lord is with you,
it is at that point that you are equipped of God to get through
any trial. In the church, we always think of Joseph as someone
who had divine favor, but in reality, it was God with him that
caused him to gain favor. When you prosper, it is then that
people begin liking you. It is then that the doors of opportunity
open. As a result, the blessing was on Joseph.

*"The blessing of the Lord, it maketh rich, and he
addeth no sorrow with it."*

Proverbs 10:22

*"A faithful man shall abound with blessings..."*

Proverbs 27:20

Joseph worked 13 years under that which was another
man's before he was given his own. David worked 13 years,
faithfully tending to that which was another man's—before

55

God gave him his own Kingdom. The prophet Elisha loyally followed Elijah for many years before receiving his mantle. Jacob served his uncle for 14 years before receiving his own flock. The Prophet Samuel served under Eli for many years before getting his own ministry. The prophet Daniel served under multiple kings of Babylon before being made governor over Babylon. The list goes on and on. What am I saying? I'm saying that leadership comes with much training and diligent working. Those that are faithful to another man's leadership will be those that God will use. The new generation of ministers and dream chasers have forgotten this. Don't expect the big before you specialize in the small. The Bible clearly states that the Kingdom is ruled by faithfulness, or steady progression. The Bible says..."first the blade, then the ear, AFTER THAT the full corn..." (Mark 4:28).

I wanted to be a preacher so bad, I would dream about it over and over again. It got so bad that my wife got sick of church and religion, because I was at church every time the church doors opened. I would turn on the television and see great men of God, and say, "I want to do that!" Yet, I didn't realize the faithfulness it took to get to the level they were at. Even Jesus had to grow.

> *"And Jesus INCREASED in wisdom and stature, and in favour with God and man."*
>
> Luke 2:52

God is exalting ministers and Kingdom-leaders who are faithful in this hour. Faithfulness is character! One day I inquired of the Lord and He spoke to me saying, "You will become a minister by measure…" As I pondered His Word, I realized that the Lord was giving it to me little by little. One day at a time. One serving at a time. The Lord was being careful not to abort my calling by giving me too much, too fast. The same happened to Joseph. His father, I believe, transgressed the will of God, by giving Joseph too much, too soon. The Lord had to start again by bringing him down to Egypt so that he could learn to serve, and thus humble himself enough to realize the value of small beginnings. For if Joseph continued in his father's inheritance, he would have been an arrogant, self-serving leader. Servant hood has a way of breaking you.

> *"Beloved, I wish above all things that thou mayest prosper and be in health, even as thy soul prospereth."*
>
> III John 1:2

The scripture says that the Lord was with Joseph, and as a result he prospered (Genesis 39:2-4). Yet, in III John 1:2, we see a connection between one's soul prospering and one outwardly prospering in the natural realm. Thus, Joseph not only prospered, but his soul grew OVER TIME in God, and as a result, he prospered outwardly. In other words, as he matured in God's Word, he prospered.

> *"This book of the law shall not depart out of thy mouth; but thou shalt meditate therein day and night, that thou mayest observe to do according to all that is written therein: for then thou shalt*

*make thy way prosperous, and then thou shalt*
*have good success."*

Joshua 1:8

Joseph grew in God because he meditated in God on a consistent basis. His mind was planted in the scriptures. As a result, the trauma and emotional scars that he received from dealing with his brothers, and the world around him were healed enough so that he was released to do his job with excellence. We see this in the prophecy that his father gave him, mentioning that Joseph "rested in the strength that does not fail him" (Genesis 49:24). All too often we are hurt by those close to us in such a way that stunts our emotional growth. These emotional arrows of rejection, strife, character assassination and betrayal so impair us that we are unable to operate in a career path or follow our dreams. If we are to follow and OBTAIN our dreams, then it is required of us to immerse ourselves in the Word of God. It heals our souls. For the Word of God is God's mind in the earth. Notice, it was a part of the dream of Joseph to be promoted over his brethren, yet if he had not been planted in the Word of God, his dreams would have never came to pass.

> *"The law of the Lord is perfect, converting the*
> *soul: the testimony of the Lord is sure, making*
> *wise the simple."*

Psalms 19:7

The Word of God heals the soul. It restores our mind, will and emotions against those traumatic events that take place in our lives. Joseph prospered because the Lord (i.e., The Word) was with him. It is important for the Word to be with you as you walk towards your destiny. The Word of God is needed in order for you to complete the race. I write this because the race is a marathon, an Ironman marathon, which you will have to sustain long periods of energy exertion. There will be heart-wrenching events that will take place. There will be traumatic events that take place. The Word will be able to heal those wounds and scars.

## Josephs Must Endure Sexual Temptations

> *"And it came to pass <u>after these things</u>, that his master's wife cast her eyes upon Joseph; and she said, Lie with me. But he refused…"*
>
> Genesis 39:8-9

The scripture says, "After these things…" It wasn't until after the promotion came that Potiphar's wife cast her eyes upon Joseph. Why wasn't this woman trying to get Joseph when he was a slave? Joseph was good looking and favorable before the promotion. Why now? Satan will do one of two things. He will attack you when you have decided to do something new, or he will attack you when you are about to reap from being faithful to a decision. Satan knew of Joseph's tendency to pride. He knew that Joseph was weakest when he was at the top of his game. We know this, because of Joseph's self-glorification before his brothers threw him into the pit. Yet, Joseph was not only faithful in duty, but he was faithful in spirit, as well. He was a man of upright, integrity. He refused to sleep with his master's wife. The mantle of Joseph is a mantle of temperance. Not temperance from the sense of never having sex, but temperance from the sense of not committing sexual acts outside of the laws of God. Joseph was a man of purity. Now, that doesn't mean he didn't lust, but it does mean he did not fall. If we are to walk fully in the end-time anointing of Joseph, then we are called not to be pulled into sexual matters that are contrary to the Word of God. The mantle of Joseph carries with it a strong requirement not to lay down in adultery or fornication. It is an end-time ministry of purity in a world of perversion. Joseph was handsome for women to admire. Ancient Egyptian women were known for their beauty, and Joseph was surrounded by them. Therefore, there was a real temptation for Joseph everywhere he went.

I know it seemed like Joseph did everything perfect, but the truth of the matter is that there had to be a struggle with lust present in him. He was human. I say this first, because the Bible says that he was a "goodly" person. The Hebrew word for goodly literally means to have beauty; be greatly beloved; to covet; delectable, great delight; desire; goodly; lust. In other words, Joseph was sexy. When women looked upon him, they saw him as one who was someone pleasing to the eye for pleasurable pursuits. As a result, I'm sure Joseph struggled with lust in himself. He desired, but couldn't touch. Now, I know the religious people reading this are saying in their hearts, "Nah! Not Joseph. He was God's elect. He was a faithful man!" I say this not in the sense of Joseph struggling with the actual act of falling in sexual sins, but the struggle with the actual temptation, itself. It wasn't as if lust didn't affect Joseph. Joseph was fine, and I'm sure women round about him made advances on him continually. We see this even in scripture, as Potiphar's wife tempted him constantly (Genesis 39:10). Thus, the desire to fall was probably an ever present struggle within him—especially if Joseph was a growing man saving himself for marriage. It can be deduced that other Egyptian women noticed Joseph, and may have even made appeals to him. He even may have had a weakness for them. I say this because, he later married an Egyptian woman (Genesis 40:50)—even though he was a Jew, and his father's tribe was living with him. He could have taken a Hebrew woman. Lastly, we also know that Satan won't tempt you with something you don't struggle with. In other words, the devil will not bring an opportunity to sin before your face unless there was a possibility of you giving in to the temptation. If your struggle is alcohol, then Satan will entice you to go to the bar. If your struggle is women, then he will create opportunities to place you before sensuous, beautiful women.

> *"But every man is tempted, when he is drawn away OF HIS OWN LUST, and enticed..."*
> James 1:14

Potiphar's wife symbolizes women of this world system, not the church system, who have success, but refuse to follow the ways of God in marriage vows. This type of woman will always try to entice a Joseph, because he stands for Godly purity and uprightness. Men with a Josephic-type of anointing are men of strong uprightness and purity. They contain powers of resistance in sexual dealings—though they struggle with temptation. They may desire to give themselves over to the lustful advances of a beautiful woman, but they resist.

## Joseph Loses Another Garment

> *"⁶And [Potiphar] left all that he had in Joseph's charge and paid no attention to anything he had except the food he ate. Now Joseph was an attractive person and fine-looking. ⁷Then after a time his master's wife cast her eyes upon Joseph, and she said, Lie with me. ⁸But he refused and said to his master's wife, See here, with me in the house my master has concern about nothing; he has put all that he has in my care.*
>
> *⁹He is not greater in this house than I am; nor has he kept anything from me except you, for you are his wife. How then can I do this great evil and sin against God? ¹⁰She spoke to Joseph day after day, but he did not listen to her, to lie with her or to be with her. ¹¹Then it happened about this time that Joseph went into the house to attend to his duties, and none of the men of the house were indoors. ¹²And she caught him by his garment, saying, Lie with me! But he left his garment in her hand and fled and got out [of the house].*

> Genesis 39:6-12 Amplified

Here we go again. Joseph finally gets to the place where he is prospering and temptation comes. His humility is tested, and he once again fails to give glory to God. Instead he praises

himself by telling his master's wife that none is greater in his
master's house than he. If anything, this reflected Joseph's attitude, showing to Potiphar's wife how he thought in his heart.
"If it wasn't for me, your husband wouldn't be as prosperous as
he has become!" This was the hidden statement of Joseph as
he claimed that there was no one as great in his master's house
as he was. I believe that this infuriated Potiphar's wife, because this was told to her as she enticed him to bed. The fact of
his loftiness before an Egyptian woman was displayed, coupled
with the fact that he refused her, probably infuriated her. How
can this Hebrew slave refuse the woman of the house, and pro-
claim that he was higher in authority than she was? She was
the master's wife. She gave the orders while her husband was
away. He mocked her status by proclaiming his own, and not
God's (Genesis 39:9).

> *"There is none greater in this house than I...And*
> *it came to pass, as she spake to Joseph day by*
> *day, that he hearkened not unto her, to lie by her,*
> *or to be with her. "*
>
> Genesis 39:9,10

> *"...See, he hath brought in an Hebrew unto us to*
> *mock us..."*
>
> Genesis 39:14

Here again we see pride rising up in Joseph. He acted in
presumption by saying, "There is none greater in this house
than I." He forgot about his master in this statement. Joseph
truly rose from being an obscure slave to being set over all that

his master had, yet in his exaltation he forgot about his servant hood, realizing that all his master obtained was his. This is just like if one was ministering before the Lord at church, and they began to realize and see that the greatness of the anointing that was on their life was not God's, but their own. It is written that pride comes before a great fall (Proverbs 16:18). This same thing happened to Lucifer, who saw his own greatness, and didn't realize that the greatness he had was given by the Father.

> *"How art thou FALLEN from heaven, O Lucifer, son of the morning! How art thou cut down to the ground, which didst weaken the nations. <u>For thou hast said in thine heart</u>, I will ascend into heaven, I will exalt my throne above the stars of God: I will sit also upon the mount of the congregation, in the sides of the north: I will ascend above the heights of the clouds: I will be like the most High."*
>
> Isaiah 14:12-14

The thing to notice is what Lucifer said in his heart. He made a decision to exalt himself. His exaltation was premeditated. Likewise, those with the Josephic mantle must be careful not to praise themselves, or give themselves the glory -as all glory goes to God. It must be remembered that Joseph praised himself, saying that none was higher than him in his master's house (Genesis 39:9). This was the mistake of Lucifer. Lucifer, in this New Testament age, represents a spirit in the church. It must be remembered that Lucifer was a cherub that covered the very throne of God. He ministered to God before the very arc of the covenant. He understood the very glory of God, and because Lucifer understood the glory of God, he began to see the brilliance and illumination of the Shekinah as his own, and not God's. This is the very essence of pride, for it turns a man's eyes inward, allowing him to see the glory that God has laid upon him as his own—not God's. Those with the mantle of Joseph must be cautious of this spirit, because it is a mantle that has been given the very access to God's throne—which is the fullness and weightiness of the Shekinah. In God's throne is the very splendor and majesty of God, Itself, even His secrets and revelations. Thus, when this Majesty is placed on those with the mantle, pride can set in, deceiving the person into thinking that this Majesty was the work of his own hands, and not God's. This was the fall of Lucifer.

> *"The Word of the Lord came again unto me, saying, Son of man, say unto the prince of Tyrus, Thus saith the Lord God; Because thine heart is lifted up, and thou hast said, I am God, I sit in the seat of God, in the midst of the seas; yet thou art a man, and not God, though thou SET THINE HEART AS THE HEART OF GOD: Behold, thou art wiser than Daniel; there is no secret that they can hide from thee: With thy wisdom and with thine understanding thou hast gotten thee riches, and hast gotten gold and silver into thy treasures: By thy great wisdom and by thy traffick hast thou increased thy riches, and thine heart is lifted up because of thy riches."*
>
> Ezekiel 28:1-5 KJV

Notice, the prince of Tyrus speaks of a man with a Lucifer Spirit. This is an actual stronghold, or strongman that often needs to be dealt with in spiritual warfare. He is a man that has the spirit of wisdom and revelation so strong that it brings him great riches and vast sums of wealth. Yet, he has exalted himself too high, calling himself God. In his great understanding he forgot God and got deceived, thinking that his understanding was the work of his own hands, and not God's. This is a demonic spirit that Satan has set over governments and ruling authorities in this hour. Now, Joseph was set by God to be exalted into the government of Pharaoh to be a covering for Israel. Pharaoh called himself a god (Isaiah 31:3), yet he was a man. We see that the same spirit of Tyrus worked and ministered throughout the Ancient Egyptian government. As a result, the Lord needed to keep Joseph humbled so that this spirit would not transfer unto him. Since Joseph was sold out to God, the Lord saw fit to continually humble Joseph when he began to move in pride and arrogance, thinking that he, himself wrought promotion over his own life. The Lord allowed the temptation of lust, through Potiphar's wife, not to test just his faithfulness, but his humility also. Joseph passed the faithfulness test, but failed the humility test, proclaiming that he was the greatest in his master's house. I believe strongly that Potiphar's wife would not have tempted him if he had not risen to be high-servant over the house of Potiphar. I say this, because the Bible clearly says that after Joseph's promotion Potiphar's wife laid eyes on him.

One thing that stands out is the fact that Potiphar's wife took his garment. Wasn't this the first thing that was taken from him when he mocked his brothers with the dreams God gave him? There is a prophetic connection, here. Potiphar's wife could have just let bygones be bygones and said nothing. But, she took the garment and laid it up so as to have compelling evidence to prosecute Joseph; to get him out of her husband's house. She was angry with him. She wanted revenge, just like his brothers wanted revenge. The first thing that was taken from Joseph was his garment. Wasn't this the same issue with his brothers? Didn't they take the coat of many colors? This, too, was a garment; a mantle; a symbol of his office and place among his brothers as well as the servants of Potiphar's house. And like his brethren, she cast him into bondage.

> *"And it came to pass, when Joseph was come unto his brethren, that they stript Joseph out of his coat, his coat of many colours that was on him."*
>
> Genesis 37:23 KJV

> *"And she caught him by his garment."*
>
> Genesis 39:12 KJV

> *"...And Joseph's master took him, and put him into prison, a place where the king's prisoners were bound: and he was there in the prison."*
>
> Genesis 39:20 KJV

> *"Come, and let us sell him to the Ishmeelites... And the Midianites sold him into Egypt unto Potiphar, an officer of Pharaoh's, and captain of the guard. "*
>
> Genesis 37:27,36 KJV

## All Things Work Together for the Good

Joseph's arrogance again led him into bondage. Those with the mantle of Joseph will many times be tested in humility. Their arrogance and presumption, or what seems like arrogance and presumption, will get them into trouble. However, the Lord has a plan. Joseph was not called to stay high-servant of Potiphar's house, for this would not be the fulfillment of the prophetic dream that God gave him. He was called to be a king; a prince over Egypt. For in his dream the sun, moon and stars all bowed before him (Genesis 37:5-11). The hosts of heaven, symbolic of multitudes of people, were commissioned by God to submit to him. How would this be brought about if Joseph was the mere high-servant of Potiphar? No, the Lord had a greater path for Joseph. So likewise, those with the Josephic-anointing will find that often their mistakes will stumble them into the path of destiny.

An example of this in my life was when I was at a season of failure and inability to excel. It seemed like the Lord was allowing every strategy in hell to come against me. Satan was attacking my career. He was attacking my marriage. He was attacking my manhood. He was attacking my finances. He was attacking everything that I held dear—my status in essence. The Lord allowed Satan to strip me of my "garment." Yet, I stayed faithful to God, attending church consistently and striving to live holy. After losing my job as a Financial Analyst, I decided to change careers. I found joy in education and blessing the youth. One day the Lord spoke to me, asking me to unite pastors to pray over the city's youth. Being obedient to the word of the Lord, I managed to unite city commissioners, multiple city directors and many pastors to help me plan a prayer event in the heart of the city. Many organizations donated money for my cause, allowing me to have enough to finance a second event in the coming year. Moreover, the city even donated the use of a public gathering memorial to host the prayer event.

In the planning of the city prayer event, a donor stepped forward to donate items to make the event fit a different vision. I warned the donor that if they were going to do this, then we would not pay for these items in any way, and that they would have to purchase them, personally. The donor agreed. The event took place and many prominent people showed up and participated in the prayer movement, including well known individuals within the state and city government, as well as nationally known individuals in education. It was a success from a spiritual and organizational standpoint. I did what the Lord asked, and blessed the children, uniting many great pastors along the way. Needless to say, I received a phone call from a marketing company a couple of months later looking for the person who purchased the items for the event. Apparently, the donor who donated the items for the event paid the marketing company with bounced checks. The donor was nowhere to be found, and since I was the convener of the event, the marketing company came after me. I got sued, even though I never signed a contract or spoke with the marketing company's owner before the event took place. After many months of fighting the lawsuit, the company realized that they did not have a case, and moved for dismissal. The amount I was being sued for was tens of thousands of dollars. At the council of my lawyer, I settled out of court for a very small fraction of the amount in question. I wanted to fight the case, but to secure my position I agreed to the settlement rather than dragging the case out into court and sparing members of my planning team any further embarrassment. Needless to say, the donor who made the purchases fled, never being accountable to what was done.

The event was a great victory on many fronts, and what seemed like a failure turned into a great success. I connected with multiple pastors, found a job, became a board member of a city-wide prayer movement, asked to serve on the intercessory team of an international, Christian organization, and most importantly, I found a church home and became planted after many years of moving from church to church. What seemed like a failure, was, in actuality, a set up by God.

> *"...And Joseph's master took him, and put him into prison, a place <u>where the king's prisoners were bound</u>: and he was there in the prison."*
> Genesis 39:20 KJV

Likewise, for Joseph, what seemed like a failure, in reality, was a set up by God. He was being divinely placed into position for advancement. He was placed into a prison of royalty. As he rose through the ranks of Potiphar's house, I'm sure young Joseph served some prominent men. Potiphar was a prominent man in the court of Pharaoh. There was probably many nights Potiphar hosted meetings of great importance at his home concerning the state of Pharaoh's army or national security, where Joseph was able to serve and meet people. When Joseph was thrown into prison, I'm sure he was confident his credibility was all but destroyed in the eyes of these people. This prison was not a normal prison. It was a prison where people who did "white collar" crimes entered. It was prison, but a prison with "perks." The Lord was setting Joseph up for a wonderful advancement, allowing him to network and connect with people who rubbed elbows with those of the royal court. I'm positive Joseph didn't see it this way until after being let out. Joseph had the opportunity to network, and he didn't even realize it. Never despise your failures, for if you are called of God, the Lord will often use your afflictions and storms to bring about wonderful pleasure and paradise. As stated before, God is a master chess player. Often in the game of chess, a retreat is actually an advancement. Joseph's backwards movement into the prison was, in reality, a positional move for the greatest promotion of his life. Joseph's prison experience was a place of transition.

> *"The steps of a good man are ordered by the Lord: and he delighteth in his way. Though he fall, he shall not be utterly cast down: for the Lord upholdeth him with his hand."*
> Psalms 37:23-24

> *"And we know that all things work together for good to them that love God, to them who are called according to his purpose...For whom he did foreknow, he also did predestinate to be conformed to the image of his Son...Moreover whom he did predestinate, them he also called: and whom he called, them he also justified: and*

*whom he justified, them he also glorified…What*
*shall we say to these things? If God be for us, who*
*can be against us?"*

Romans 8:28-31

Even though Joseph was being cast into bondage for a second time, he was in the right place at the right time. How strange is that? How can you be in prison and have it be considered a right position at the right time; at the right place? I'm sure Joseph was discouraged all the time not realizing that God had divinely positioned him. Joseph did what was right in the sight of the Lord by refusing to sleep with his employers wife. Yet, he was in prison. Have you ever done what was right in the sight of the Lord, but caught hell as opposed to reward? Have you ever did the right thing, but received what seemed like a demotion, as opposed to a promotion? Don't worry, the Lord has your feet. He will keep your foot from stumbling, even when it seems like you are going backward for doing the right thing.

*"Be not afraid of sudden fear, neither of the*
*desolation of the wicked, when it cometh. For the*
*Lord shall be thy confidence, and shall keep thy*
*foot from being taken."*

Proverbs 3:25-26 KJV

We cannot worry at times of great challenge, because when we are doing right and bad comes our way, we must know that God is working it for our good. We must remind ourselves that God is in control, and that He is the Lord of the path of our feet. He will position us for the right promotion. Joseph was not called of God just to stay at Potiphar's house. He had to resist Potiphar's wife to be thrown into prison that God could bring him to the palace.

# 3

## Joseph's Obedience

### The Bitterness of the Mantle

*"Many are the afflictions of the righteous: but the Lord delivereth him out of them all."*

Psalms 34:19 KJV

If God gave you a dream, then don't give up on that dream. It must be realized that great affliction comes with a dream. Great warfare is involved in the unlocking of that dream out of heaven. Joseph had a dream—literally—but because of his dream he fell into great warfare, bondage and affliction. There will be many times that it will look like your dream will never come to pass. I'm sure when Joseph was thrown into prison, he thought to himself that his dream would never come true. I'm sure when Joseph was made a servant in Potiphar's house, he thought to himself that he would never become anything but a slave. The mantle of Joseph comes with much affliction; much humbling and much serving. Contrary to popular belief,

75

it is not a mantle of ease. It seems like Joseph's life was one of ease. It seems like Joseph did everything right. It seems like he worked effortlessly and got promoted. It seems like everyone favored him. Yet, there was a 13-year period between the prophecy and the promise. The Bible says that Joseph's enemies sorely grieved him (Genesis 49:23). In the Hebrew this means, literally, to make bitter. The Hebrew word used for bitter is a derivative of the word, Marah. This word was used in connection to the children of Israel at the waters of Marah, where God turned the bitter waters sweet (Exodus 15:23).

I often hear ministers teach about how Joseph didn't get bitter, because he forgave his brothers. In actuality, Joseph did get bitter, according to scripture. For the Bible says that his enemies made him bitter by sorely grieving him. As a result, we know that the mantle of Joseph is a mantle of bitterness. In other words, it's a mantle that will cause you to have to deal with bitterness, because people will fight your dream. It is a mantle and a gifting that causes people to become jealous of you, not just for what you are called to do, but also for the multitude of gifts (i.e., coat of many colors) that God has given you. People will curse you. They will try to hinder your progress. They will talk about you. They will overlook you. They will try to sabotage you on the job and in the church. They will hate you merely because you are gifted. This, in turn, will often make you bitter at them, finding it harder to forgive. When you are sitting in your prison, which is prophetic symbolism for the bondage your enemy seems to have successfully put you in, you begin thinking about what they did to facilitate you getting to the place you are at. Joseph struggled emotionally. Its obvious. His own brothers, whom he loved, sold him into slavery. They orchestrated a plan to bring him under the attack of Satan. Do you not know that your enemies will use witchcraft to see you fail? I'm sure Joseph became bitter at Potiphar's wife—who lied on him. She conceived a plan of revenge that stripped him of his position and office, that resulted in him being put into prison. Has anyone ever hated on you so bad that you lost your job? Has anyone been so jealous of your prosperity that they tried to bring you into poverty? Has anyone hated your marriage so much that they tried to bring about a divorce? Welcome to the mantle of Joseph. Afflictions and bondage bring bitterness. Joseph had his fair share.

The beautiful thing about this is that God will make your bitter experience sweet again. He has promised this in His Word. The Lord will deliver you out of every affliction. He has promised it in His Word. It is up to us to stay in the fight. Don't backslide. Don't throw your hands up and say, "Man, forget this Christianity crap!" I cannot tell you the number of times I just gave up on God, but the Lord wouldn't allow me to quit. I'd go to church, get afflicted, and then give up, only to have the Lord preach to me a Word on not giving up. I never forget one day I got really discouraged with my former pastor. I wanted to go into ministry, but he was very abusive, and many of his actions angered me. At the time I worked at a major grocery store here in the area. So, after church I went to work—mad. I was so discouraged with my dream of being a minister that I threw in the towel right then and there. Yet, not a second after I told myself to give up, I saw an Energizer Battery advertisement that said, "...Still going. It keeps going and going and going and...." At that point the Lord spoke to my heart to say, "You can't give up. You have to keep going and going and going and going!" So likewise, when the battle gets fierce, and you find your soul scarred, it is at that point that you have to push yourself to keep going. Joseph could have gave up in that jail. Yet, he encouraged himself in the Lord and served the prisoners.

## Prophetic Revelation & Dream Interpretation

Now, Joseph was an interpreter of dreams. He was blessed of God to help bring dreams to pass. He brought dreams out of the spiritual realm to make them tangible and understandable by interpretation. He helped peoples' dreams come true through interpreting the dream and giving insightful. Those with the mantle of Joseph have a gift not only to interpret the dreams of others—i.e., make them tangible and coherent—but also to help carry out those dreams. This is why Josephs' specialize in the ministry of helps and serving. They are equipped by God to interpret the dreams of others, as well as carry it out. Now, to interpret is to give or provide the meaning of something; to explain; elucidate; to understand in a particular way; to bring out meaning. Those with the Joseph mantle are programmed by God to interpret what others are called by God to do, and help them bring the vision to pass through servant hood.

When a man with the Joseph-mantle begins to interpret your dream (i.e., assignment from God), he is simultaneously fulfilling his dream. We see this all throughout Joseph's life. As he served the vision of others (Potiphar, the king's servants, and Pharaoh) he himself was promoted by God, and used to cover Israel (i.e., the church) in a time of great famine.

It all starts with a dream.

> *"And they dreamed a dream both of them, each man his dream in one night, each man according to the interpretation of his dream, the butler and the baker of the king of Egypt, which were bound in the prison."*
>
> Genesis 40:5

God is truly the divine orchestrator. God has a way of setting us up to see if we have learned from our own mistakes. Despite Joseph's consistent failure to give God glory for his gifts, He still brings Joseph the opportunity to learn from his mistakes. God moves Potiphar's wife to envy Joseph for refusing her sexual advances, and then moves Potiphar, himself, with anger to throw Joseph into prison. Next, the Lord allows Potiphar to place him in the same prison that royal officials go to when they transgress against the king. Lastly, he gives both of the king's officials a dream *on the same night*, so that Joseph can interpret both dreams the next morning when he walks into their cell to serve them. This is all divine providence. Notice, Joseph was just on his normal serving routine. He was making his rounds, serving. Yet, he stumbled unto destiny. The Bible says that a man's gift will make room for him (Prov 18:16). I have found an even more profound principle. A man's gift will make room for him when he is found faithful. Joseph would have never had the opportunity to minister to these men if he was not in the prison, or working diligently. Yet, this time, Joseph learned his lesson. He gave glory to God, and not himself.

*And Joseph said unto them, Do not interpreta-*
*tions belong to God? Tell me them, I pray you."*

Genesis 40:8

Do you remember when Joseph boasted his dreams to his brothers? Do you remember when Joseph arrogantly presumed he was set over Potiphar's house? Each time he exalted himself, the Lord humbled him. How? The first time he exalted himself through his gift, his brothers sold him into slavery. The second time he exalted himself, his master put him into prison. Each time Joseph was humbled, it was done by conspiracy and deceit. The young Joseph was beginning to learn his lesson. He was maturing. He was beginning to realize the flaw in self-exaltation, and the wisdom of giving glory to God. It was finally dawning on Joseph that whatever he obtains; whatever he becomes; whatever he is able to do with his hands or mind, it all comes from God. This was the gist of everything Joseph was going through. This was the whole point of his trials—his slavery; his prison experience. The Lord was teaching him that there was nothing he could do that the Lord didn't give him strength to do. The Lord was preparing him for greatness. Joseph was finally growing into his mantle.

> *"And the chief butler told his dream to Joseph,*
> *and said to him, In my dream, behold, a vine was*
> *before me; And in the vine were three branches:*
> *and it was as though it budded, and her blos-*
> *soms shot forth; and the clusters thereof brought*
> *forth ripe grapes: And Pharaoh's cup was in my*
> *hand: and I took the grapes, and pressed them*

*into Pharaoh's hand. And Joseph said unto him, This is the interpretation of it: The three branches are three days; Yet within three days shall Pharaoh lift up thine head, and restore thee unto thy place: and thou shalt deliver Pharaoh's cup into his hand, after the former manner when thou wast his butler. But think on me when it shall be well with thee, unto me, and make mention of me unto Pharaoh, and bring me out of this house."*

Again, Joseph was a prophet. He interprets dreams. The Lord speaks to prophets through visions and dreams, and meeting the Lord in dreams is one of the various prerequisites of one with the prophetic gifting.

*"And the Lord came down in the pillar of the cloud, and stood in the door of the tabernacle, and called Aaron and Miriam: and they both came forth. And he said, Hear now my words: If there be a prophet among you, I the Lord will make myself known unto him in a vision, and will speak unto him in a dream."*

Numbers 12:5-6

*"If there arise amoung you a prophet, or a dreamer of dreams..."*

Deuteronomy 13:1

*"The prophet that hath a dream, let him tell a dream; and he that hath my word, let him speak*

81

*my word faithfully. What is the chaff to the wheat? Saith the Lord."*

Jeremiah 23:28

*"For God speaketh once, yea twice, yet man pre-ceiveth it not. In a dream, in a vision of the night, when deep sleep falleth upon men, in slumbering upon the bed; Then he openeth the ears of men, and sealeth their instruction."*

Job 33:14-16

I strongly believe that those of the Josephic gifting are those who understand God through the unraveling of dreams. It must be understood that dreams from God are spoken to man through riddle. If God speaks to man in dreams, then God hides His revelatory glory in that dream so that the man can understand God more fully by the patient perseverance it takes to seek God for the unlocking of that dream. For example, Daniel fasted for three weeks to find out the interpretation of a dream. In other words, he searched God out copiously for understanding.

*"In the third year of Cyrus king of Persia a thing was revealed unto Daniel...and the thing was true, but the time appointed was long: and he understood the thing, and had understanding of the vision. In those days I Daniel was mourning three full weeks. I ate no pleasant bread, neither came flesh nor wine in my mouth, neither did I anoint myself at all, till three whole weeks*

*were fulfilled...Then said he unto me, Fear not,*
*Daniel: for from the first day that thou didst set*
*thine heart to understand, and to chasten thyself*
*before thy God, thy words were heard, and I am*
*come for thy words."*

Daniel 10:1-3; 12

Dreams are interpreted while visions are open, needing no interpretation at all. When a man can interpret a dream, then it speaks to the strength of that man's prophetic ability.

*"...It is the glory of God to conceal a thing: but*
*the honour of kings to search out a matter."*

Proverbs 25:2

Understanding and interpreting the mysteries of God is a kingly function. There is a Kingdom-type glory associated with it. It also speaks to the man's wisdom and discreetness. A prophet who can unlock the mystery of dreams have strong prophetic knowledge and **kingly authority**, being enabled by God to fathom the language of heaven, which is often knowledge too high for the flesh. Joseph displayed this ability in a powerful way, because all throughout his life he understood and unlocked mysteries. Those of the prophetic mantle of Joseph are gifted in the knowledge and interpretation of revelation, dark sayings, parables, harbingers and mysteries. They have a prophetic gifting to understand parables and apostolic knowledge. This comes about by intense seasons of study, and through knowledge of the scriptures. Dreams and visions are a world unto themselves. This knowledge, then, qualifies those with the Josephic mantle to operate in kingly authority. We see this in scripture with Peter, who is given authority to lock and unlock those things that are treasured up within the kingdom of heaven.

> *"He saith unto them, But whom say ye that I am? And Simon Peter answered and said, Thou art the Christ, the Son of the living God. And Jesus answered and said unto him, Blessed art thou, Simon Barjona: for flesh and blood hath not revealed it unto thee, but my Father which is in heaven. And I say also unto thee, That thou art Peter, and upon this rock I will build my church; and the gates of hell shall not prevail against it. And I will give unto thee the keys of the kingdom of heaven: and whatsoever thou shalt bind on earth shall be bound in heaven: and whatsoever thou shalt loose on earth shall be loosed in heaven."*
>
> Matthew 16:15-19

In the scripture above, we read that Peter was given the keys to a kingdom. Who has keys to a kingdom? A king, right. Revelation is a kingly function, or characteristic. Those that labor diligently and painstakingly to obtain it will qualify themselves for a kingly ministry, function or office. It must be remembered that Jesus said that the "kingdom of heaven suffers violence, but the violent takes it by force" (Matthew 11:12). Those that have power over the Kingdom of Heaven are those that seize it and take it by force. The words of Jesus almost give the impression that the Kingdom of Heaven is up for grabs, and that anyone who seeks to have it gets it by violent, ardent and zealous effort. I believe strongly that the Lord is speaking about authority. We know from study that authority is given to kings, right (Proverbs 25:2)? What I'm trying to teach you is that the Kingdom of Heaven is ruled by authority. It revolves around authority. It is operated by authority. It functions on the sole principal of authority. A kingdom is a king's realm. It is the territory of a king, right? So, it is ruled by the king on the divine principle of his authority as a king. So likewise, when God gives us keys to a kingdom, He is giving us the authority to access His kingdom at will. Access to the Kingdom of Heaven is the ability to operate in authority as a king in the earth—having authority over situations by bringing Heaven into that situation through spiritual knowledge. If one is going to access a spiritual kingdom, which is a kingdom that is not seen by the carnal eye, then one needs divine insight into how that kingdom operates. This divine insight is given through revelation. The Kingdom of Heaven is higher than the Kingdom of the earth. In other words, the heavens will always rule over the earth. This is why Jesus said, "Thy KINGDOM come. Thy will be done on earth as it is in heaven" (Matthew 6:10). Therefore, when we move in revelation we move in authority over the earth realm, walking as kings, bringing heaven into the earth. When revelation is given by God, then authority, simultaneously, is transferred to the one that has obtained this understanding to operate in kingdom dominion. This is why most prophets in the Old Testament usually had authority over kings, making kingdom-decisions that affected the whole nation of Israel. We see this in the life of Isaiah, having authority over Hezekiah; Elijah having authority over Ahab; Nathan having authority over David (II Sam 12); and Samuel having authority over Saul. Revelation is used for the purposes of bringing divine and Godly answers to the realm of the earth, establishing Heavens rule over it. It is used to solve earthly problems that can only be unlocked by heavenly answers. Those that obtain it take authority in the earth, having power over nations as kings.

## To God be the Glory: A Glimpse of Maturity

As in the life of Joseph, we see that his powers of revelation in interpreting the dream of two of Pharaoh's officials brings him before the king, himself. The Pharaoh has two dreams and none could interpret them.

> *"Then spake the chief butler unto Pharaoh, saying, I do remember my faults this day" Pharaoh was wroth with his servants, and put me in ward in the captain of the guard's house, both me and the chief baker: And we dreamed a dream in one night, I and he; we dreamed each man according to the interpretation of his dream. And there was there with us a young man, an Hebrew, servant to the captain of the guard; and we told him, and he interpreted to us our dreams...And it came to pass, as he interpreted to us, so it was... Then Pharaoh sent and called Joseph, and thy brought him hastily out of the dungeon."*
>
> Genesis 41:9-14

Joseph was brought before the Pharaoh when the Lord took him through a pruning process. He finally came to the end of himself, realizing that his gift was not for him, but given to him by the grace of God. It wasn't until Joseph began giving God the glory for his gift that the Lord began opening doors for him.

> *"...And Pharaoh said unto Joseph, I have dreamed a dream, and there is none that can interpret it: and I have heard say of thee, that thou canst understand a dream to interpret it. And Joseph answered Pharaoh, saying, It is not in me: God shall give Pharaoh an answer of peace."*
>
> Genesis 41:15-16

Joseph is finally getting it! At first, when in jail after exalting himself, he encounters men, and has the opportunity to exalt God for the gift that is inside him. When he does this, the Lord acknowledges Joseph's humility by bringing him before the king. Now, Joseph stands before a king and he remembers all his trials and tribulations. He remembers why he had to go through what he went through. Instead of directing Pharaoh to his own ability to interpret dreams, Joseph abruptly corrects the king by showing the king that his ability is given to him by God, and that God alone gives him the ability to interpret dreams.

> *"...I have heard say of thee, that thou canst understand a dream to interpret it. And Joseph answered Pharaoh, saying, It is not in me: God shall give Pharaoh an answer of peace."*
>
> Genesis 41:15-16

God in His glorious wisdom and sagacity, programs a fail-safe in the mantle of Joseph. In order for the gift to be activated and translated into purpose, those with the mantle of Joseph must be careful to give glory to God for the gift. If you fail to do this, then you will stay in bondage. You will never move forth into purpose. The doors will stay closed until it dawns on you to bless God with your gift and not yourself. Joseph became obedient through those things that he suffered, and with that experience learned that God truly is the Lord of lords and the King of kings. God is the creator and ruler of Eternity, and time exists in Eternity.

So, what happens next in our story? Joseph goes on to interpret Pharaoh's dream, showing Pharaoh that God is the true giver and revealer of dreams. After interpreting these dreams, the very thing that Joseph's brothers stripped from him was returned to him seven times greater. The first thing Pharaoh does is promote Joseph and put upon him a newer, refined mantle—the mantle of Joseph.

> *"And Pharaoh took off his ring from his hand, and put it upon Joseph's hand, and arrayed him in vestures of fine linen, and put a gold chain about his neck."*
>
> Genesis 41:42

His brothers stripped him of his mantle because of his gift to interpret dreams, and Pharaoh restored unto Joseph a **double portion** of the mantle for submitting his gift to God. After we go through the process of understanding the sovereignty of God, He will restore double unto us that which was taken.

All through the story of Joseph, every time God changed his position, he changed his garments. He brothers stripped him of the coat of many colors, speaking prophetically of a shift in position, and Joseph goes into slavery. Potiphar's wife stripped him of his garments, prophetically speaking of another shift in position, and Joseph goes to jail. Finally, Pharaoh arrayed him in vestures of fine linen, symbolizing yet another positional shift, and Joseph becomes the governor of Egypt. Whenever God was about to change Joseph's position, He would change his garments—his mantle. The coat of many colors of Jacob foretold the garments that Joseph was to where in the house of Pharaoh. The mantle that Pharaoh placed upon Joseph was the restoration of the true, complete mantle that was originally foreseen by the dream Joseph had at 17 years old.

Joseph had come full circle. The Lord humbled him, pruned him and then turned around and exalted him. In the pruning process he learned how to become a servant, being faithful to all that the Lord put him over. His obedience won the day. However, the story wasn't over. All his serving under Potiphar trained him and qualified him for the next level God was about to give him.

## Authority & Wisdom Comes With The Josephic-Revelation

When we move in revelation the Lord also gives wisdom and authority to bring the revelation to pass. What do I mean? When the Lord trusts us with His revelatory ability, He also gives us wisdom and authority to carry out what He shows us. For example, if the Lord gives a person a dream about how something should be fixed in another person's life, He will also give that person who had the dream the ability to fix it. This could be through disclosing the dream, or entering into the situation and rectifying it directly. Right alongside revelation is authority, or ability, to establish that which was revealed. We see this in the life of Peter, who had a personal revelation of who the Lord was to him.

Matthew 16:

>  *16Simon Peter replied, You are the Christ, the Son of the living God. 17Then Jesus answered him, Blessed [happy, fortunate, and [d]to be envied] are you, Simon Bar-Jonah. For flesh and blood [men] have not revealed this to you, but My Father Who is in heaven. 18And I tell you, you are [e]Peter [Greek, Petros—a large piece of rock], and on this rock [Greek, petra—a [f]huge rock like Gibraltar] I will build My church, and the gates of Hades [the powers of the [g]infernal region] shall [h]not overpower it [or be strong to its detriment or hold out against it]. 19I will give you the keys of the kingdom of heaven; and whatever you bind (declare to be improper and unlawful) on earth [i]must be what is already bound in heaven; and whatever you loose (declare lawful) on earth [j]must be what is already loosed in heaven.(B)*

After Peter had a revelation given to him, Jesus authorized, or gave him authority to operate that which was revealed to him. Understand, then, because Peter had a revelation, he was able to go forth in the earth and establish that revelation. He was given keys –authorization; authority. We know that Christ is the Word. When we recognize and understand who Christ is, we understand and recognize what the Word is. As a result, the Word is disclosed to us through revelation. When we have a personal revelation of the Word[Christ], we are then given authority to establish the Word[Christ], unlocking the mystery of the Word [Christ] out of heaven, into the earth-realm in order to solve problems, or bring the wisdom of Heaven to situations. This brings about a two-fold blessing:

**1. It breaks the curse of Adam**—Man having to toil by the sweat of his brow, using his carnal understanding to solve the troubles of this world, must toil to figure things out. Yet, revelation brings a spiritual answer to an earthly problem, circumventing having to figure things out by natural means.

**2. It advances/promotes the bearer of the revelation**—He is now charged with the responsibility of solving the problem through Divine assistance, bringing glory to God.

God wants His eternal answers in the earth, so that the curse that came upon Adam will be reversed. This is only done through the Word of God (Christ), which can only be unlocked through revelation. Also, more than not, he uses the person to whom the revelation was given to establish the answer. We see this in the life of Joseph. Once the enigma of the dream was revealed to Joseph (it wasn't revealed to Pharaoh), God gave him wisdom to advise Pharaoh on what to do. Pharaoh, then, realizing that Joseph was a man of understanding through God, gave Joseph authority to carry out this wisdom.

*"Now therefore Pharaoh look out a man <u>discreet</u> and <u>wise</u>, and set him over the land of Egypt. Let Pharaoh do this, and let him appoint officers over the land, and take up the fifth part of the land of Egypt in the seven plenteous years. And let them gather all the food of those good years that come, and lay up corn under the hand of Pharaoh, and let them keep food in the cities. And that food shall be for store to the land against the seven years of famine, which shall be in the land of Egypt; that the land perish not through the famine. And the thing was good in the eyes of Pharaoh, and in the eyes of all his servants. And Pharaoh said unto his servants, Can we find such a one as this is, a man in whom the Spirit of God is? And Pharaoh said unto Joseph, Forasmuch as God hath shewed thee all this, there is none so discreet and wise as thou art.*

*Thou shalt be over my house, and according unto thy word shall all my people be ruled: only in the throne will I be greater than thou."*

Genesis 41:33-40

Through this scripture we see the two-fold blessing taking place. God used Joseph to bless the whole land of Egypt, therefore breaking the curse of the law that came about through Adam. God also advanced Joseph, promoting him and setting him under Pharaoh to be Viceroy over Egypt. Had Joseph not been obedient to the process of serving Potiphar, he would not have been qualified to serve Pharaoh. The Lord blessed the whole house of Potiphar, for Joseph's sake. Therefore, God blessed the whole land of Egypt, the house of Pharaoh, for Joseph's sake. Those with the mantle of Joseph are called to do the same thing. The gift given to the mantle is not only revelation, but wisdom, being graced by God to solve problems. The Josephic mantle has the wisdom and discreetness of God to counsel the oracles of God to kings, so that kings are able to rule easier and wiser. The mantle of Joseph is a governmental grace used to give God glory in answering world problems such as famine, death, war and prosperity. Like Joseph, those with this mantle are given powers of revelation and authority to establish heaven on earth. This is done by being placed in positions of authority to be a blessing to authority, as well as those who come under its rule. We see this also in the life of Daniel, the prophet, after he interpreted Nebuchadnezzar's dream.

*Forasmuch as thou sawest that the stone was cut out of the mountain without hands and that it brake in pieces the iron, the brass, the clay, the silver, and the gold; the great God hath made known to the king what shall come to pass hereafter: and the dream is certain, and the interpretation thereof sure. Then the king Nebuchadnezzar fell upon his face and worshipped Daniel, and commanded that they should offer an oblation and sweet odours unto him. The king answered unto Daniel, and said, Of a truth it is, that your God is a God of gods, and a Lord of kings, and* <u>a revealer of secrets</u>, *seeing thou couldest* reveal this secret.

*Then the king made Daniel a great man, and gave him many great gifts, and made him ruler over the whole province of Babylon, and chief of the governors over all the wise men of Babylon."*

Daniel 2:31-36; 44-48 KJV

As soon as Daniel gave the interpretation of the dream, it was perceived by the king that the Spirit of God was in Daniel to understand dreams and visions, and therefore to rule with wisdom. Nebuchadnezzar gave Daniel, like Joseph, rulership over the land, making him Viceroy, thereby bestowing, with Daniel's revelation, the authority to carry it out. Whoever has revelation has rulership and authority to carry out what was revealed.

*"And Pharaoh called Joseph's name Zaph'nath-pa-a-ne-ah..."*

Genesis 41:45

When we study the meaning of the name that was given to Joseph, we see that the meaning of the name is "revealer of secrets." Notice, the king saw the gift in Joseph to interpret

secrets, yet had Joseph never went through the process of being humbled and serving to build his integrity, the king would
have never discerned in him the ability to rule the country. So,
let the process process you.

# 4

# The Prophesies of Joseph

*"Joseph is a fruitful bough, even a fruitful bough by a well; whose branches run over the wall: the archers have sorely grieved him, and shot at him, and hated him: But his bow abode in strength, and the arms of his hands were made strong by the hands of the mighty God of Jacob; (from thence is the Shepherd, the stone of Israel:) Even by the God of thy father, who shall help thee; and by the Almighty, who shall bless thee with the blessings of heaven above, blessings of the deep that lieth under, blessings of the breasts, and of the womb: The blessings of thy father have prevailed above the blessings of my progenitors unto the utmost bound of the everlasting hills: they shall be on the head of Joseph, and on the crown of the head of him that was separate from his brethren."*

Genesis 49:26 KJV

This book would not be incomplete if we don't process what Biblical prophecy has to say concerning Joseph. Let's look at the first prophecy concerning Joseph pronounced on him by his father, Jacob. I spent many years referring to these prophesies, because they spoke to my life in so many ways. The mantle of Joseph is a generational blessing. What I mean by this is that those graced with this gifting and manner of blessing is usually given it by way of those that came before them in their family tree. One thing that I noticed is that my family members have a Josephic-type blessing on them. In other words, its generational. Its an anointing that is passed down the family tree. Let's analyze Jacob's prophetic message.

> *1. "Joseph is a fruitful bough, even a fruitful bough by a well; whose branches run over the wall:"*

The prophesy in Genesis goes on to foretell and prophetically decree the main theme of Joseph's life, even the life of those with the Josephic blessing. The Bible says that Joseph is a fruitful bough. When researched in the Bible, a fruitful bough in the concordance refers to Joseph as one who builds the family name. It also refers to the word "bough" as meaning one who is ***afflicted***; ***a young bull***; an anointed one; firstborn; child; **servant born**; **steward**; worthy; **young one; youth**. All these words describe a "bough" in the Hebrew language. Moses, when he described the Josephic mantle, was using a "bough," which is a tree or branch in modern language, to speak to the reader that those with this mantle are those who will have to suffer affliction as the firstborn. When I say firstborn, I don't mean firstborn in the sense of being the first to come out of the womb. We must think of firstborn as one whom the Lord ratifies His covenant with. Those with the mantle of Joseph are those whom the Lord has made covenant with as a firstborn son. In ancient times, the firstborn was the one with the greatest, or largest inheritance. Likewise, those with the mantle of Joseph are those sanctified of God to have the largest inheritance among his/her siblings, as a firstborn son. They will have a youthful spirit, or anointing. They are those people anointed of God to steward and be servant-born children of God. Remember those that would be great are called to be servants among his brethren (Mark 23:11).

> *"...even a fruitful bough by a well; whose branches run over the wall:"*

Whenever I get a little discouraged I often refer to this phrase of scripture. One of the Hebrew meanings of bough is "afflicted one." Those with the anointing of Joseph will come up against opposition. This opposition will be in the form of a wall. Walls are erected to stop progress. Many enemies will try to oppose your growth through jealousy and envy, because you are fruitful and prosperous. Yet, the Lord said that Joseph's branches ran over the wall. In other words, every affliction and enemy that will try to oppose you, the Lord will cause you to overcome. Joseph's branches grew over the wall, because he was a bough planted by a well. The thing about wells is that they tap into groundwater far underneath the surface. Trees that grow by wells tend to flourish because they have a root system that tap into the same ground water system that the well does. Therefore, the writer of this prophesy was informing the reader that Joseph's root system was deeply planted into the ground so as to access a fresh and plentiful supply of water to grow and become fruitful thereby. Thus, the wall was overcome by the branches of the tree in the growth process.

Joseph was anointed for affliction. In other words, when affliction came, he was able to access the Spirit of God—symbolic of the ground water of the well—to overcome, or over-grow walls (opposition). What does that say to those with Joseph-type mantles? It says that located in this gift is the ability to tap deep into the presence of God to tackle insurmountable odds. Notice, the wall was not necessarily overcome, it was overgrown. Those with the mantle of Joseph are given the ability to transcend, or mature past, the walls, or issues trying to stop growth, in their lives because they have a fresh supply of the Word (symbolic of water) in their foundations (roots systems) that people can't see.

> 2. *"the archers have sorely grieved him, and shot at him, and <u>hated</u> him: But his bow abode in strength, and the arms of his hands were made strong by the hands of the mighty God of Jacob; (from thence is the Shepherd, the stone of Israel:) Even by the God of thy father, who shall help thee; and by the Almighty, who shall bless thee with the blessings of heaven above, blessings of the deep that lieth under, blessings of the breasts, and of the womb."*

The Bible says that many are the afflictions of the righteous, but the Lord delivers him out of them all. We see in this section of the prophetic word that Joseph was shot at by his enemies. The archers sorely grieved him AND shot at him. When we think of archers, we think of the words of people. The word hate in the Hebrew literally means to persecute. When one is persecuted, it means to pursue with harassing or oppressive treatment because of beliefs; to harass continually. If you look up "hate" in the Strong's Biblical Concordance it is almost in the same pronunciation as the word, Satan, which means to accuse. Hate also means to lurk. When we think of the verb, to lurk, it means to conceal oneself as if to ambush. So we see that with the mantle of Joseph comes much persecution for the sake of the cross. Joseph was accused, persecuted and harassed for the sake of his pursuit of the dream. When you follow after the footsteps of Joseph, you will be persecuted, accused and harassed by Satan, through people, because you pursue after that which the Lord has called you.

The archers shot at Joseph and grieved him. Joseph had haters, for the Bible says that archers hated him. This hatred grieved, or distressed, Joseph. The word grieve means to suffer mental distress or feel sorrow for something—i.e., depression. Yet, the Bible says that his bow—which is the bow of a bow and arrow—abode in strength. This word strength means to continue; to be hard; to be permanent. Thus, the writer of the prophecy was painting a picture of a war that was taking place between Joseph and his enemies. Imagine a war with archers on one side and archers on the other. The archers against Joseph grieved him, yet Joseph remained steadfast in shooting arrows back, and thus remained strong. Joseph didn't faint. He kept sure and strong in God. He remained steadfast in the midst of adversity.

> *"and the arms of his hands were made strong by the hands of the mighty God of Jacob; (from thence is the Shepherd, the stone of Israel:) Even by the God of thy father, who shall help thee; and by the Almighty, who shall bless thee with the blessings of heaven above, blessings of the deep that lieth under, blessings of the breasts, and of the womb."*

Many times our battles that we fight are the battles that hinder our finances. They test our character. They test our faith. We see in this part of the prophecy that Joseph had a generational blessing that undergirded him. It helped him to succeed. This goes back to the main subject of this prophecy, which says that Joseph was a tree planted by a well. The generational blessing of Joseph was the help of the God of his father. The same help that God gave Jacob was the same help that God gave Joseph. This help was the blessings of heaven— the spiritual blessing of God's presence. The blessing of the deep—the blessing of the earth which yield prosperity. The blessing of the womb—the blessing of children and offspring. We see that these things come into play when Joseph's enemies hated on him. When Satan comes to attack you, the blessings of your forefathers and foremothers will kick in, and you will be strengthened by the same thing that strengthened them, which translates into putting your trust in God the same way your ancestors did.

*3.  "The blessings of thy father have <u>prevailed</u>
above the blessings of my progenitors unto the
utmost bound of the everlasting hills:*

Jacob, who gave the prophecy to Joseph, said that his
blessing was upon him. The word that was interesting to me
was the word, "prevailed." Jacob was given a blessing by God
to prevail. The word prevail means to be or prove superior in
strength, power or influence. Prevail also means to succeed or
win out. Now, it was through the blessing of Jacob that Joseph was able to win in the battle against those that sorely
grieved and hated on him. This happens not in a quick fight,
but in the contest. Joseph was able to out-endure his enemies.
His enemies fought against him, but he served the Lord more
steadfastly. Jacob was given this same blessing.

*And he said, Thy name shall be called no more
Jacob, but Israel: for as a prince hast thou power
with God and with men, and hast prevailed.*

Genesis 32:28

Jacob wrestled with God, the Bible says, and prevailed.
What is the prophetic symbolism of this scripture? How can a
man wrestle with God and win? It is obvious that God allowed
Jacob to win, but it speaks more to Jacob wrestling with his
own flesh, overcoming it and being wounded by God in the process. Often, certain things are not loosed out of heaven easily.
What do I mean? When we wrestle with situations and issues,
the solution of those things don't get released out of heaven
easily. There is a perseverance and a wrestling that has to

take place before the Lord releases that thing. Jacob wrestled with an angel, who represented God. This same strength, the Bible says, was found in Joseph, who was able to harness the blessing of his father and wrestle with situations and circumstances until he received of God the answer he needed. The Lord will, on purpose, hide His divine answer/blessing, so that you will have to lean on Him—prophetic of a wrestling with your flesh—in order to loose that thing out of heaven. Joseph prevailed at this, because the scripture says that his bow remained strong, or steadfast.

4.  ...they shall be on the head of Joseph, and on the crown of the head of him that was separate from his brethren."

When I first read this passage, I thought that the writer was referring to Joseph's crown as an actual crown a king would wear, but proper analysis of this scripture would actually reveal that the crown of Joseph's head meant the top of his head. As a result, when we think of the crown of Joseph's head, it would be proper to think of an anointing being poured out on top of his head. Therefore, the prophesy would represent a type of anointing, ability or mantle that Joseph was given of God. He was a brother who was separate from his brethren. In other words, he wasn't one who easily fit in. Even when Joseph was young, being 17 years old, he wasn't easily accepted of his brethren, because of the type of mantle or anointing that God gave him. People who have the mantle of Joseph are people who don't easily fit in. They must fight through rejection. They tend to be socially awkward. People can be easily offended by them, because they tend to seem independent of the group. Yet, the blessing of the Lord is on the head of people, as an anointing or gifting, that possess the mantle of Joseph.

## Second Prophecy of Joseph

Deuteronomy 33:

> *[13]And of Joseph he said: Blessed by the Lord be his land, with the precious gifts of heaven from the dew and from the deep that couches beneath, [14]With the precious things of the fruits of the sun and with the precious yield of the months, [15]With the chief products of the ancient mountains and with the precious things of the everlasting hills, [16]With the precious things of the earth and its fullness and the favor and goodwill of Him Who dwelt in the bush. Let these blessings come upon the head of Joseph, upon the crown of the head of him who was separate and prince among his brothers.[B] [17]Like a firstling young bull his majesty is, and his horns like the horns of the wild ox; with them he shall push the peoples, all of them, to the ends of the earth. And they are the ten thousands of Ephraim, and they are the thousands of Manasseh.*

This second prophecy is about the blessings of Joseph, and is very similar to the blessing that Jacob pronounced on Joseph in Genesis. The Bible is emphasizing the importance and blessing of the Josephic mantle. We know that the Bible was written for our admonition and direction. We can look at the Word and use the word for our own lives. As with Joseph, his life, and his prophecies is a guide for our life. What am I saying? I am saying that those of you with the blessing of Joseph on your life can take these promises as your own promises. You have a Joseph-type blessing on your life, and these prophecies define what type of blessing it is.

*1.  And of Joseph he said: Blessed by the Lord be his land*

This statement defines the whole foundation of the Josephic blessing and mantle. Blessed be Joseph's land. Blessed be his heart. It is important to see the Bible in terms of types. When I say types, I say archetypes. The dictionary defines an archetype as the original pattern or model of which all things of the same type are representations or copies: PROTOTYPE; *also*: a perfect example. So, things in the Old Testament have become spiritual types of that which is in the New Testament. We see this when the bible talks about Jezebel.

*But I have this against you: that you tolerate the woman Jezebel, who calls herself a prophetess [claiming to be inspired], and who is teaching and leading astray my servants and beguiling them into practicing sexual vice and eating food sacrificed to idols.*

Revelation 2:20

In this scripture we see that the New Testament speaks of Jezebel, but Jezebel is an Old Testament figure, having died in the scripture through being thrown off a palace balcony (2 Kings 9:33). Yet, how can John the revelator write about a New Testament church suffering the woman Jezebel, who was killed thousands of years before? The Bible was referring to her spirit. So likewise, one can have the spirit of David as one can have the spirit of Jezebel. One can have the spirit of Elijah as one can have the spirit of Judah. Thus, one can have the spirit of Joseph. In our case we call it the mantle of Joseph. This is all done through Christ.

When we talk about land, as with Josephic prophesy, the New Testament prophetically refers to land as a man's heart, just like bread is prophetically symbolic of the word of God. We see this in scripture:

Mark 4:
*14The sower sows the Word. 15The ones along the path are those who have the Word sown [in their hearts]*

The scripture above speaks about the ground, or land, as a type or symbol of the heart. The parable of the sower is about a farmer who sows seed into the land. Jesus is then asked by his disciples why He speaks to his outer circle in parables. He tells them that He conceals, or hides, truths in the form of parables, a story of symbols and types, so that only the truly devout can understand. He then goes on to decode the parable to his inner circle:

Mark 4 (Amplified)

> [10]And as soon as He was alone, those who were around Him, with the Twelve [apostles], began to ask Him about the parables. [11]And He said to them, To you has been entrusted the mystery of the kingdom of God [that is, [b]the secret counsels of God which are hidden from the ungodly]; but for those outside [[c]of our circle] everything becomes a parable, [12]In order that they may [indeed] look and look but not see and perceive, and may hear and hear but not grasp and comprehend, [d]lest haply they should turn again, and it [[e]their willful rejection of the truth] should be forgiven them.[(A)] [13]And He said to them, Do you not discern and understand this parable? How then is it possible for you to discern and understand all the parables?

Are you getting it? The whole bible is a parable in many ways. It hides interpretive truths that can only be understood by those who know God and seek Him through study. Additionally, there are many things in the Old Testament that translate into prophetic symbols in the New Testament, land being one of them.

As a result of the parable, we see that the land was a spiritual metaphor, or representation, for the heart of a man. I have to lay this groundwork in order to make you fully understand the blessing of Joseph, for Moses prophesied concerning Joseph, "Blessed by the Lord be his land." What does this mean metaphorically, or should I say, prophetically? It means that Joseph was a man whose heart, or soul, was blessed by the Lord. Joseph was a 100-fold hearer of the word. God blessed his heart to bring forth fruitfulness in the earth. As stated before, those who are like Joseph in the church are those whom the Lord has blessed their heart. When your heart is blessed, your actual, literal land will be blessed as well.

> *20And these are they which are sown on good ground [Hearts]; such as hear the word, and receive it, and bring forth fruit, some thirtyfold, some sixty, and some an hundred.*
>
> Mark 4

Joseph was a hearer and doer of the Word of God. Joseph had a good heart! As a result, the Lord gave him increase.

> *13And of Joseph he said: Blessed by the Lord be his land(heart), with the precious gifts of heaven from the dew and from the deep that couches beneath, 14With the precious things of the fruits of the sun and with the precious yield of the months, 15With the chief products of the ancient mountains and with the precious things of the everlasting hills, 16With the precious things of the earth and its fullness and the favor and goodwill of Him Who dwelt in the bush.*

Since Joseph's heart was so blessed, the Lord made all that he did to increase and grow. One of the words that stuck out to me in this prophesy was the word, "precious." What does precious mean, and why was Moses referring to Joseph as a precious person? It seemed to be the defining factor of Joseph's ability to bring forth fruit. The dictionary defines precious as something that is of high price or great value; very valuable or costly; highly esteemed for some spiritual, nonmaterial, or moral quality; affectedly or excessively delicate, refined, or nice. The Strong's Concordance defines precious in the scripture as Meged [meh-ghed], which means to be eminent; a distinguished thing; something valuable like a product or fruit; pleasant; precious fruit. Therefore Joseph was not only anointed of God to bring forth fruit, but to bring forth fruit most preciously. Joseph was a man of value and worth through the blessings of God.

You need to take this as your identity and inheritance. You need to declare that the Lord has blessed you with the blessing of Joseph, and that you are empowered of God to produce preciously in the earth! Those with the mantle of Joseph are anointed of God to not only produce or create, but to produce and create preciously in the earth. The blessing of Joseph is one of increase—valuable, refined and costly increase. When the Bible speaks of fruitfulness, it is referring to increase and bountifulness.

2. *"...and the favor and goodwill of Him Who dwelt in the bush."*

When the Bible speaks of favor, it is literally speaking about grace. When we study grace, we find that grace and favor are one. In order to understand the mantle of Joseph, we cannot forget the favor of God. We think of how the Lord favored Joseph. Those with the mantle of Joseph have the favor of the Lord to increase; to bring forth preciously and valuably in the earth. The favor of the Lord has come not from man, but from the Lord. When you have the blessing of Joseph on your life favor and goodwill will come from God. This is favor and goodwill in business transactions. This is favor and goodwill from people who will bless you. This is favor and goodwill on your children. This is favor and goodwill on everything you touch.

> 3. *"Let these blessings come upon the head of Joseph, upon the crown of the head of him who was separate and prince among his brothers."*

What does this mean? Remember David? Remember when he was anointed in the midst of his brothers? Well, this blessing is like it. Those with the mantle of Joseph will have to go through affliction and persecution at the hand of their brothers and sisters in Christ, because of the anointing and blessing of increase on their lives. We know that Joseph's brothers threw him into a pit, because they hated him. Well, when the blessing of Joseph comes upon you in its fullness, the Lord will turn around and allow those same brothers and sisters to see you exalted. Joseph's brothers had to behold the prophesy come to pass in his life. The folks who treated him cruelly had to now watch him be blessed and highly favored of God. The blessing and mantle of Joseph will cause your enemies to have to watch you succeed. They will see you go down, but they will see you also go up.

This same characteristic must be used when obtaining the blessing of Joseph. We are to love our enemies and bless them. When this happens, the Lord, in due season, blesses us in such a way that our enemies will have to behold our success. The minute we become cruel and vindictive to those we call our enemies, the Lord will keep us from promotion until we learn this principle. Joseph forgave his enemies. As carriers of the blessing of Joseph, it is our mandate before God to love our enemies, especially when the Lord gives us an opportunity to do to them what they have done to us.

4. *17Like a firstling young bull his majesty is, and his horns like the horns of the wild ox; with them he shall push the peoples, all of them, to the ends of the earth.*

We know from the prophecy about Joseph in the book of Genesis that one of the meanings of "bough" was young bull. Well, in this portion of the scripture we see this same prophetic word, literally. Joseph is likened to a young bull or ox. An ox in the Bible is the prophetic symbol of servant hood and strength. It is also an apostolic animal, or a symbol of the apostolic ministry. One thing about oxen is that they have horns. Horns are the symbol of authority that speak of power and ability. The prophesy says that with his horns he will push, gore or make war against the people to the ends of the earth. What does this mean? This speaks to how Joseph will defend himself against his enemies. We see a definition of this in the book of Psalms.

*Through You we will push back our adversaries;*
*Through Your name we will trample down those*
*who rise up against us.*

Psalm 44:5

Joseph was likened to a bull in scripture that was able to push back his enemies with his horns, or authority. The Bible says that Christ has given us authority, or power, to tread upon serpents and scorpions. We have been given power and authority, by way of the mantle of Joseph, to push back the demonic attacks of the enemy.

# 5

## Joseph & Daniel—
## Governmental Prophets

There is one other person in the Bible who had an eerily similar ministry to Joseph. This person was the Prophet Daniel. Daniel was called to Babylon to help it administratively in order to set in place the initiative to rebuild Israel. He was divinely placed within a world system in order to cover the church, as Joseph. His ability to understand and know secrets is what gave him room before kings, yet it was his faithful character that allowed him to sustain his position among the princes of Babylon. We see this same similarity in Joseph, who had a gift for understanding the secrets of God, as well as having Godly character to sustain him among the princes of Egypt.

The similarities between Joseph and Daniel are staggering, and not beyond the scope of this book. What is noteworthy is that Daniel, though gifted administratively, was gifted of God in the prophetic realm. The bible says that he excelled in understanding visions and dreams.

*As for these four children, God gave them knowledge and skill in* **ALL** *learning and wisdom: and Daniel had understanding in* **ALL** *visions and dreams.*

Daniel 1:17

What stands out is that the scripture says that God gave Daniel "knowledge and skill in ALL learning and wisdom." This is where the administrative side comes to fruition. Daniel gained his great prophetic acumen through passionate study of God's law and knowledge. It must be understood that Daniel was gifted, like Joseph, in the realm of revelation. Revelation only comes by way of study. David underscores it best in the Psalms.

*I have more understanding than all my teachers: for thy testimonies are my meditation.*

Psalm 119:99

It is only right to deduce that Daniel was well gifted in administration due to his great intellectual properties, and therefore easily picked out of the crowd of Hebrew exiles to serve in the court of the Babylonian king. His original job function was to teach.

*Children in whom was no blemish, but well favoured,* **and skilful in all wisdom, and cunning in knowledge, and understanding science, and such as had ability in them to stand in the king's palace,** *and whom they* *might teach the learning and the tongue of the Chaldeans.*

Daniel 1:4

In order to be skillful in knowledge, one must know how to teach. A perquisite of a teacher is one who understands knowledge. You cannot fully understand anything unless you know how to teach it to others. Daniel had this ability. These traits closely match those of Joseph, who also had powers of prophetic insight and understanding of administration.

More detail on Daniel and Joseph is beyond the scope of this book, and will be analyzed in another work. Below is a table I constructed that highlights the striking similarities of both Joseph and Daniel. This suggests that both these men had the same mantle or gifting. They were prophets called to deal with world governments, affecting the way governments legislated policy within the current world system. In reality, they changed the world through their prophetic gifts and abilities. Yet, they both were children of Israel. Israel speaks to us prophetically of the church. Therefore, Joseph and Daniel are end-time, church mantles or gifting, called of God to be a covering for the church in these times.

| Attributes | Joseph | Daniel |
|---|---|---|
| Interpreter of Dreams | Interpreted the Dream of Pharaoh | Interpreted the Dream of Nebuchadnezzar |
| Slavery | Was put into slavery by brothers | Was put into exile (slavery) |
| Understood Servant hood | Served in the Egyptian Court | Served in the Babylonian Court |
| 2nd in Command | Became Viceroy over Egypt, second to only Pharaoh | Became governor of Babylon, second only to King of Babylon |
| Same Names | Given an Egyptian name: Zaphnathpaaneah = "Revealer of Secrets." | Given a Babylonian Name: Belteshazzar = " Bel is the keeper of Secrets." |
| Same Gifting | Promoted through revelation | Promoted through revelation |
| Leadership | Managed the wealth of Egypt | Managed state affairs in Babylon |
| Ministry | Gifting in Governments and State Management through Prophetic revelation | Gifting in Governments and State Management through Prophetical revelations |
| Support to Church (Israel) | Protected Israel in drought | Influenced the release of Israel from Exile |

| Attributes | Joseph | Daniel |
|---|---|---|
| Character | Faithful to Serve Potiphar and Pharaoh | Faithful to serve Kings of Babylon |
| Distinction | Knew the Lord through Dreams | Knew the Lord through visions and dreams. |
| Modern Day Career | Economics; Management; Leadership; Finance; Government | Economics; Management; Leadership; Government; Diplomacy |

# Locating the Joseph Mantle:
# A Cheat Sheet

How do you know you have the mantle of Joseph? What are the signs and attributes? Below is a chart that highlights the attributes of those with the Josephic mantle.

| ATTRIBUTES | ABILITIES |
| --- | --- |
| Spiritual Gifts & Traits | Discerning of Spirits; Gift of Prophecy; Word of Knowledge; Word of Wisdom; Seer; Revelator; Oracle; Understanding; Revelation; Favor |
| Prophetic Sign | The Glory of God; The Bull; Young Bull; Ox; Another Word for Cherub is Ox (Ezekiel 10:14) |
| Name Meaning | Zaphnathpaaneah = Revealer of Secrets (Genesis 41:45) |
| Five-fold Ministry Gift | Apostle: The Prophetic sign of the Apostle is the Bull; an apostle is a higher prophet with greater authority.<br>Prophet : Is a governmental gift; sees and interprets the mind of God. |
| Career | Secular: Governments; Business; Marketplace Ministry; Financial Manager; Treasurer; Church: Janitor; Church Servant; Gatekeeper; Porter; administrator; |
| Modern-Day Assignment | Solve Problems in Government; Corporate Systems and Church Systems. Governmental Leadership and Management; Called to serve Leadership; Called to interpret and carry out the dreams of others. In doing so, will cover Israel (Modern-Day Church) from disaster and calamity. |

| | |
|---|---|
| Skills | Multi-Tasking; Management; Leadership; Servant-Leadership; Strong Work Ethic; Faithfulness; Integrity; Intelligence; Those of the church usually, but not always, taught through higher education and church simultaneously. |
| Character | Fidelity; Faithfulness; Integrity; Honesty; Uprightness; Generosity; Forgiveness; Compassion; Mercy. |
| Prophetic Number | 4 = Number of Double (2+2; 2 X 2); Number of Four Corners of Earth; Number of the Cherubim (4 faces); Number of Creation (North, South, East, West); Number of Elements (Air; Water; Fire; Earth); Number of the Season (Winter; Spring; Summer; Fall); |

# The Prayer of Joseph

"Father God, I thank You for making me faithful like Joseph. My heart is blessed. My land is blessed. I walk in the precious glory of God. I thank You that You have made me fruitful. I am creative and prolific. What I put my hands to prospers and has good success. Lord, You have gifted me to multiply and be creative in the earth realm. My creativity brings me wealth and increase. I'm productive, and the productivity of my hands produces precious substance. There is great value on my creative works. Lord, cause me to mature and grow past the walls and blockades my enemies set up against me to stop me. I have an unction from God to out-endure my enemies. Everything they throw at me, I will overcome. I prevail against the snares and traps of my enemies. I will out grow and out produce the wiles of the devil and the schemes of my enemies. Father, I thank You that You exalt me before my enemies, because I walk in love towards them, and everything they meant for evil, You will turn around for my good. My works abide in strength by the grace of God. You will cause all those that meant evil for me to have to witness my rise and exaltation. Father, I thank You that You promote me before my enemies and those that wish me harm. I'm blessed with the precious things of heaven and earth. Precious is my fruit brought forth by the sun. Precious is my produce brought forth by the moon. My produce is precious. My production is precious. The work and output of my hands is precious. The goodwill of heaven is upon my head. I have the favor and mercy of the Most High. It is You, O Lord, that makes me strong. With the authority You have given me in prayer, I will push back my foes and Satan's strategies are reversed.